Relax, It's Just Sex

Relax, It's Just Sex

Understanding Non-Possessive Intimate Relationships

Leslie Spurr, PhD

Enjoy!

Les

PRAEGER™

An Imprint of ABC-CLIO, LLC

Santa Barbara, California • Denver, Colorado

Library of Congress Cataloging-in-Publication Data

Names: Spurr, Leslie, author.
Title: Relax, it's just sex : understanding non-possessive intimate relationships / Leslie Spurr, PhD.
Description: Santa Barbara, California : Praeger, [2017] | Includes bibliographical references and index.
Identifiers: LCCN 2017002097 (print) | LCCN 2017015824 (ebook) | ISBN 9781440854743 (ebook) | ISBN 9781440854736 (hardback)
Subjects: LCSH: Non-monogamous relationships. | Sex. | Sexual freedom.
Classification: LCC HQ980 (ebook) | LCC HQ980 .S68 2017 (print) | DDC 306.7—dc23
LC record available at https://lccn.loc.gov/2017002097

ISBN: 978-1-4408-5473-6
EISBN: 978-1-4408-5474-3

21 20 19 18 17   1 2 3 4 5

This book is also available as an eBook.

Praeger
An Imprint of ABC-CLIO, LLC

ABC-CLIO, LLC
130 Cremona Drive, P.O. Box 1911
Santa Barbara, California 93116-1911
www.abc-clio.com

This book is printed on acid-free paper ∞

Manufactured in the United States of America

To my research assistant, Lois.

Contents

Introduction

In this book, I describe a relatively new form of relationship style that appears to be increasingly prevalent among contemporary couples and singles.

In this bold new world, both men and women, and especially married couples, are discovering that they no longer need to demand sexual exclusivity as the essential requirement of a committed relationship. The insight, which has come to most of these adventurous couples, is that sexual fidelity may not only be unnecessary but possibly not even desirable in a long-term bonded relationship.

This revelation has created somewhat of a social/sexual reformation that has rippled across North America, Europe, and most Western countries. Starting from small numbers in the 1960s, this movement, emphasizing a non-possessive intimate relationship style, has gathered momentum, especially since the 1990s. It now represents a sizeable and well-established subculture, but one of which those in mainstream society are relatively unaware.

The purpose of this book is simply to describe this emerging phenomenon and to explain how it works, psychologically, for the couples and singles involved. As with any cultural change, new terms and concepts may emerge and, where relevant, I have defined and described these.

These nontraditional relationship styles may be expressed in many different ways and occur in several different contexts, depending on the preferences of the persons involved. I have tried to present these variations in some detail so that the reader may get a sense of the variety possible and some flavor of how these non-possessive arrangements actually work.

Although I have used male/female couples primarily for illustrative examples in this presentation, the same arrangements are, of course, utilized by many homoerotic couples. In fact, gays and lesbians pioneered these non-possessive intimate relationship styles before they became popular in the straight world.

In researching and preparing material for this book, I have functioned much like an anthropologist attempting to describe and explain, say, the mating rituals of some exotic tribe of natives. The "natives" here, however, may be your co-workers or next-door neighbors!

It is important to be aware of some significant limitations in the discussion that follows. The information and analysis presented here are not the result of a rigorous scientific survey. Investigations into people's intimate behaviors are notoriously difficult to conduct and even when attempted are often susceptible to several types of shortcomings.

The interpretations and ideas that make up this brief overview arose from several sources. Chief among these sources were my work as a couples' therapist, my review of the (very limited) relevant literature, and my direct observation of activities in these somewhat underground communities. (Ah, the joys of field research!)

In order to add a pinch of zest to the somewhat didactic descriptive material, I have included brief quotes taken from those I have spoken with as clients and interviewees. These are intended to illustrate, in more personal terms, the concepts being described and, at times, to add a touch of humor to the discussion.

In writing this book, I have tried to follow the advice of the first word in the title by adding attempts at amusement as a relaxing strategy. I hope you will be able to chuckle along with me as we poke gentle fun at all sides of this controversial issue.

This text is not intended primarily as a scholarly work. The statements made within are not buttressed by references to academic journal research or by footnotes detailing complex points of psychological theory.

As a book intended for a wider audience, it has been written to appeal to the more general reader who may have an interest in this topic. As such, the primary references I have used to illustrate and expand on the ideas being presented are to works in the popular media, such as movies, songs, novels, etc., which may be more widely known.

Like any good social scientist, I have tried to remain objective and non-judgmental, simply reporting my observations and attempting to offer plausible explanations for the dynamics of this social/sexual phenomenon. Please note that I am neither advocating nor condemning this relatively new form of coupling. I am simply describing it, FYI, with the hope that this presentation will shed light on a topic that has not been well-recognized or described previously.

I have tried to organize the material in a way that will allow the reader to best understand how non-possessive intimate relationships work. The first few chapters introduce some basic concepts. The next several chapters illustrate how these concepts are applied in various formats. The last chapters describe how those who are involved in these relationships attempt to get their needs met.

After perusing this book, many people will decide that this "new morality" is not for them. Others may be stimulated to explore these possibilities further. For those, the Notes and Bibliography may prove useful.

To all readers, I hope you will find this book both informative and entertaining and that you will enjoy reading it as much as I enjoyed researching and writing it.

CHAPTER ONE

Intimate Relationships

Exclusivity

"Wilt thou, forsaking all others, keep thee only unto him/her so long as ye both shall live?"[1]

—The Book of Common Prayer

We are all intimately familiar with how intimate relationships are supposed to work. We can't help but know the rules. From our earliest awareness, we are exposed to countless overt and covert messages from authority figures and the popular media telling us how we should meet someone, fall in love, get married, and live happily ever after, all the while being faithful to that one person.

A key element explicit in this idealized trajectory is the principle of exclusivity, i.e., one man, one woman (only!). Common wedding vow phrases, such as "forsaking all others," express this commitment to one's one and only. This exclusivity model is so pervasive in our culture and so reinforced by popular song lyrics, Hollywood movies, books, poetry, and more that positive alternatives are barely, if at all, ever mentioned.

Betrayals of the exclusivist commitment are also an integral part of the fabric of our popular culture (e.g., watch a few soap operas). Everyone is familiar with terms such as "infidelity" and "unfaithfulness," which we use to express the expected breach of trust when intimate behaviors occur with others outside of the primary relationship.

The exclusivity mandate is strongly supported by the moral arbiters of virtually all contemporary cultures. Exclusivity in relationships is generally conceded to be essential for social stability and is an unquestioned pillar of "family values" and other conservative social concepts.

Granting exclusivity to another person or demanding exclusivity from someone else brings control issues into the relationship. The prohibition against intimate involvement with outsiders reinforces the notion of regarding one's partner as one's personal property. Enforcing restrictions on another person's thoughts, feelings, or actions may be seen as defining a relationship as possessive.

But what if there was no exclusivity agreement or possessive arrangement as to sexual and/or romantic interactions with others? Is it possible that the partners in a relationship could agree that it would be acceptable to engage intimately with outsiders and still maintain the other aspects of their togetherness?

Until recently, this possibility has been considered so unlikely that it rarely has seen expression in the popular media, the teachings of our moral educators, or in any form. Consequently, for almost everyone in our culture, it is not even considered as an option.

Conjointly-agreed upon alternatives to exclusivity in intimate relationships have probably always existed, however. For example, during the so-called "free love" era of the 1960s and 1970s,[2] non-exclusive intimate relationship arrangements were popularized by the media, which often used their controversial nature to sensationalize the counterculture of that time.

More recently, we seem to have been experiencing a resurgence of interest in non-exclusive intimate relationship arrangements.[3] Over the past two decades, increasing numbers of people have been exploring swinging, polyamory, threesomes, and many other types of relationships in which, by mutual agreement, others are definitely *not* forsaken, sexually and/or romantically. The rapid growth of these alternative lifestyles and the beginnings of media attention to these activities may eventually qualify this phenomenon as a new sexual revolution.

Relationships

"Come live with me and be my love,
And we will all the pleasures prove."[4]

—Christopher Marlowe

A relationship exists if two (or more) persons think, feel, and act toward each other differently than they would toward other people. A relationship always involves some sort of agreement between/among the partners. This agreement typically specifies the ways in which each partner gives preference to the other partner(s).

The establishing agreement may be clearly specified, even written and signed, such as a pre-nuptial contract. More commonly, the relationship agreement is just verbally proposed and accepted, often in vague terms.

The agreement may include limits on the preferential treatment, including circumstances under which the special considerations may not apply. Affirmative actions may be included (e.g., "Love me forever"). Most significantly, however, the agreement typically specifies, either explicitly or implicitly, what the partners may not do, especially vis-à-vis outsiders.

Both (or all) parties need to consent to whatever agreement defines their relationship. If one does not, we have the "Girl from Ipanema"[5] situation, i.e., a one-sided love affair perhaps, but no relationship.

Both parties have to be able to commit in some way to the relationship. Thus, the concept can be stretched to include non-human entities (a girl and her horse, a Kiwi guy and his favorite sheep) but not to inanimate objects (can a surfer have a "relationship" with his board?).

An *intimate* relationship implies the involvement of at least some aspects of affection, romance, and/or sex. In these areas, the lovers in an intimate relationship think, feel, and act toward each other in ways that are special, in comparison to the ways they interact with other people.

In most traditional intimate relationships, there is a strong element of possession. Because of the restrictive aspects of their agreement, each partner usually feels some degree of ownership and/or control over the other partner's behavior and often their thoughts and feelings also.

Traditional relationships are all virtually the same in terms of how the arrangements between the partners are structured. Non-traditional relationships vary significantly, however, in the ways the participants construct their do's and don'ts agreements.

For the non-traditional relationships surveyed in this book, about the only thing that they have in common is that they all involve an agreed-upon decision by each partner to give up, at least to some degree, total possession, and thus full control, over the intimate activities of the other partner(s).

In non-possessive intimate relationships, the partners modify the traditional agreement so as to relinquish, or at least reduce, the degree of control over what each other thinks, feels, and does. People involved in non-possessive relationships tend to value individual freedoms, both for themselves and for their partners.

In our culture, we are well aware of a significant gender discrepancy in the presumed motivation to agree to committed relationships. Men are generally assumed to prefer non-committed arrangements and to want to avoid being "tied down" by any one woman (except, of course, for bondage and discipline submissives).

For a woman, the general expectation is that the goal of dating is to find her one-and-only Prince Charming and then lock him into an exclusive relationship, preferably marriage.

In reality, of course, motives regarding bonding into intimate relationships are way more complex with much gender-role crossings, at times. Nevertheless, the standard romantic-comedy screenplay, pitting the pursuing female against the commitment-shy male remains immediately recognizable to all as the defining conflict in the "battle of the sexes."

Alternatives to the Traditional Model

"Seek simplicity and then distrust it."[6]

—Alfred North Whitehead

In spite of the historical and cross-cultural pervasiveness of the bonding arrangement committed to exclusivity, there are, and probably always have been, alternative relationship styles. Hence, we come to the curious case of the consensual non-possessive intimate relationship.

Different people often understand the same words in different ways. In order to understand better these non-traditional choices, it may be helpful as a starting point, therefore, to clarify some terms and concepts.

A "relationship" could be said to exist when two (or more) people, based on their previous experience with each other, establish some mutual understanding intended to provide guidance regarding the future behavior of the partners in the relationship. This agreement may be explicit or tacit and may change over time but provides a kind of contractual commitment as to what the relationship partners should or should not do.

Relationships may exist in many forms, involving, for example, business, familial, and competitive arrangements in which people commit to certain ways of relating to each other. "Intimate" relationships imply that there is some degree of sexual and/or romantic interaction between (or among) the partners.

In "non-possessive" relationships, there may be no, or at least limited, attempts to exert control over the intimate behaviors, thoughts or feelings of one's partner. In these arrangements, there is an agreement that the relationship is not one based on the concept of ownership of the other person.

Many types of people can engage in non-possessive intimate relationships, which can exist in many different forms. For the purposes of this discussion, the primary focus is on heterosexual couples, defined as a man and a woman having some type of ongoing interaction, such as dating or marriage.

Many uncoupled people, i.e., singles, engage in non-possessive intimate relationships in the time-honored tradition of "playing the field." Gays and others of the LGBT orientation have long pioneered various forms of non-exclusive intimate relationships. For these individuals, non-possessive intimate relationships are nothing relatively new.

What is new is the evolution among many traditional straight couples into novel forms of non-possessiveness in the intimate relations between themselves and with others. These adventurous couples are tweaking the standard relationship model in new ways that, they hope, will better meet their needs.

In doing so, these unconventional couples are questioning the role of sexual exclusiveness as the sine qua non of relationship commitment. They are emphasizing the non-sexual aspects of their relationship as the more important bases for their bonding and removing sex with others as a criterion of disloyalty.

Non-possessive intimate relationships may be seen as expressions of the broader concept of the "sex-positive" movement. Being sex-positive means promoting and embracing all forms of sexuality, as long as the sex is safe and consensual.

Often attributed to Wilhelm Reich, sex positivity is an attitude that regards all mutually-agreed sexual activities as fundamentally healthy and pleasurable.[7] It is contrasted with sex negativity, which is frequently advocated by the moral arbiters of most societies. (For more on this topic, visit the Center for Sex-Positive Culture in Seattle and peruse their extensive library of resources.)

The Relationship Trajectory

"What goes up must come down."[8]

—Isaac Newton

In order to understand more clearly the choices made by those involved in non-possessive intimate relationships, it may be helpful to consider first the traditional relationship trajectory.

In its customary form, a relationship starts when two people meet and start to engage in a series of encounters with each other, e.g., dating. As a result of these encounters, there is typically some degree of physical intimacy between the individuals and some emotional attachment is formed. During these initial get-togethers, each individual may still be dating others and may have some degree of emotional and sexual bonding with these additional options.

Often, two individuals who are dating may decide at some point to make a "commitment" of some kind to each other. This commitment almost always takes the form of an agreement, which may be either explicitly stated or unspoken but clearly understood, in which each individual pledges to restrict their romantic and sexual activities with others. When this occurs, the two individuals begin to regard themselves as partners in a bonded relationship.

Generally, the essence of the commitment is that each partner agrees that (s)he will be romantically and sexually exclusive with her/his bonded partner. At that point, it is typically expected that dating with outsiders will cease and any prior intimacy or emotional commitments to others will be broken off.

The boundaries of these expectations may vary somewhat and the individuals involved may use different terms to describe their arrangement, such as "going steady," "seeing someone," and so on. In all of these committed relationships, however, there is ordinarily some (at least implicit) understanding that one's partner is valued more than others who are not one's partner. An "other" has become a "significant other."

The decision to go exclusive is an existential moment in the trajectory of a relationship. It sets the couple onto a new path, opening some doors and closing others. It redefines the former two individuals as now being a "couple." It redefines the relationship from being uncommitted to being monogamous.

The decision to couple exclusively usually arises when at least one of the single individuals involved in the dating relationship feels strongly enough about the person they are dating that they now want to bind an agreement with that person to make them and themselves contractually obligated.

The standard contract almost always has two essential clauses: 1) You will agree to refrain from any sexual or romantic involvement with others, and 2) I will agree to do the same.

These exclusiveness clauses are ordinarily seen as highly, and often the most, critical elements of the relationship. So much so that violations of these expectations are frequently considered sufficient basis for termination of the relationship.

The impetus to enter into a restrictive covenant such as this generally increases when at least one of the individuals in a dating relationship starts to have increasing concern that the person they are dating may not always be available to them. The decision to initiate and/or to enter into an agreement to restrict one's own behavior, especially behavior that may be very satisfying, is usually motivated by even stronger needs. Most often, the anxiety caused by the threat of potential loss of the other person prompts the individual to act to "lock in" the relationship.

The trajectory of a traditional intimate relationship generally moves through increasing levels of exclusiveness. Progressively greater restrictions may be proposed and agreed to as the former individuals move from "seeing" other people to considering themselves a bonded unit.

Often, the transition to exclusivity is marked by a symbolic gift of some kind, usually given by the male to the female. Pendants and bracelets to signify "going together" may lead up to engagement and wedding rings. Each of these allegorical trinkets serves to remind the partners that there is some degree of possessiveness now present in the relationship.

After the individuals agree to become a monogamous couple, their relationship may deepen and expand. They may move in together, get engaged, married, have children, etc. Concurrently, however, and at least partly due to the stresses caused by some of the above factors, exclusivity, which seemed like such a good arrangement initially, may later be seen as unduly restrictive.

Virtually all romantic and sexual relationships, whether committed or not, seem to follow a rather predictable pattern as they extend over time. The first flush of love and sexual excitement rises and peaks at some point and then starts to decline, reaching lower levels of intensity eventually. Timelines of relationship passion can vary greatly from the rapid (see the film *9½ Weeks*[9]) to the slow fade to black, familiar to most long-married couples (see *Blue Valentine*[10]).

Sometimes, the upswing can be very lengthy (see *When Harry Met Sally*[11]) and sometimes the downturn can be precipitous (see *War of the Roses*[12]). Generally, however, there is a relatively quick upward phase, often measured in weeks or months, and a slower downward trend, often measured in years, to the standard relationship trajectory.

Our fantasies may be shaped by fairy tales and Hollywood movies, but even in these fables, there is some recognition that although happiness can be everlasting, continued erotic attraction is unlikely. (How often have you seen the last line expressed as, "And they lived *passionately* ever after"?)

At some point on the downward slope, one or both of the partners to the traditional commitment agreement may begin to question the value of the relationship in meeting their needs for passion and the excitement that comes with new love.

When this happens, the couple is at another existential choice point.

To most partners in an exclusive relationship, the options at this juncture seem to be:

- Suppress erotic/romantic urges toward others, or
- Have covert affairs, or
- Dissolve the relationship and seek a new passion partner.

To the individuals involved, each of these choices may appear to have significant and somewhat predictable negative consequences.

A novel solution to this dilemma has evolved over the last few decades in which some relationship partners have discovered that it is possible to de-couple the exclusivity clause from the rest of the relationship agreement.

In this scenario, the couple may agree that intimacy and/or romance could be consensually allowable with outsiders, subject to certain negotiated conditions, but that the couple will remain together and bonded in all other ways.

This de-coupling of sex and/or romance from being necessarily exclusive to the relationship can offer several advantages to the couple. Their togetherness can continue with all of its positive benefits, including love and sex with each other. Trust and honesty can be maintained and the possible trauma resulting from illicit assignations can be avoided. Strongly felt desires, such as for passion and/or romance, need not be suppressed entirely but are given a sanctioned outlet.

The partners of a couple who have been together for a lengthy period and who have seen the intensity of their erotic feelings for each other fade with time may feel like their only options are to choose between continued love or new sex. By considering the non-possessive alternative, the couple may find they can have both.

A husband or wife may say, "I love my spouse and I make love with her/him. But, with the knowledge and approval of my spouse, I also have sex with others and this activity is separate from and does not interfere with me loving my spouse." Couples for whom this type of arrangement works well may describe it as having your cake and eating her/him too.

A Little History

When we hear, "It's still the same old story, A fight for love and glory," these lyrics from "As Time Goes By"[13] remind us that the struggle to achieve a love relationship is eternal.

In spite of the pervasiveness of the standard possessive model of intimate relationships, however, exceptions have probably always existed. One common example has been the unilateral variant in which one of the partners is free to engage sexually or romantically with outsiders and the other is not. Polygamy, harems, and the tacit "double standard" all demonstrate the ubiquity of this one-sided arrangement and illustrate its invariable gender bias toward male privilege.

Dionysian (essentially, like hedonism, a belief that all people have the right to do everything in their power to seek the greatest amount of pleasure) and other similar Greco-Roman orgiastic activities were probably also very male-controlled rather than gender egalitarian. Until the mid-20th century, there appears to have been very few instances of non-possessive intimate arrangements in any culture in which both men and women were free to choose their own external sexual or romantic partners.

Historical instances of non-possessive intimate relationships as a societal norm can be found quite readily in many Pacific Islander cultures, however. Many of the early Polynesians, for example, had relatively few restrictions on sexual/romantic involvements for either men or women.[14] This unrestricted sharing of intimacies must have been an amusing discovery to the European men of the first ships to explore destinations such as Hawaii and experience this special type of "aloha."

Truly bilateral examples of non-possessive intimate relationships, in which both partners had sexual and/or romantic freedom, have existed historically in Western culture but mainly in quasi-religious groups as part of a larger value system. The early Oneida (a religious sect prominent in the 1800s), for example, believed that all of one's possessions were to be shared equally among the group, even one's spouse![15]

In the 1960s, several factors came together to create a kind of perfect storm of cultural change causing a sexual revolution in which traditional values were challenged and new alternatives explored. Primarily in North America and Western Europe, a zeitgeist emerged that emphasized the value of free thinking in all ways and led to the adoption of unconventional relationship arrangements.

During this time, the advent of the birth-control pill greatly reduced the threat of pregnancy while the widespread use of condoms and improved antibiotics made sexually transmitted infections much less of a concern.

The rise of feminism and the women's liberation movement of the 1970s alerted many people (including even some men) to the negatives associated with the male domination imperative. Many women began to insist on the unrestricted right to choose their own sexual partners, whether in a relationship or not.

Communes and co-ops were developed, some of which featured the sharing of sexual partners among the members. Campus organizations, such as the Sexual Freedom League,[16] gave visibility to the notion of liberated sexuality. Even the anti-war movement, with its iconic slogan "Make love not war," expressed the sentiment that fornicating is better than fighting.

"Wife swapping" emerged in this era and, although still tagged with a sexist label, was probably the first fairly widespread social phenomenon in which couples exchanged partners. "Key parties" (during which men put their car keys in a bag or box and women later blindly pulled out a set to determine who they would go home with) introduced a random factor into the process, and "social clubs" were developed as meeting and greeting places for couples looking for like-minded others to negotiate trades.

The sexual revolution of the 1960s ushered in a time of permissiveness in which couples began experimenting with reducing or eliminating relationship restrictions. The notion that sex and love should be given unrestrictedly was a primary value of the "free love" era of the 1970s, a time in which many couples began to explore the concept of consensual non-monogamy.[17]

After a return to more conservative relationship values in the 1980s, the cultural values pendulum again started a swing toward the more liberal end of the continuum in the 1990s with the rise of the "recreational sex" movement. (For a good time, call up Em & Lo's humorous dictionary of rec sex terms.)[18]

In the 1990s, many urban singles opted off the traditional relationship trajectory and instead developed networks of "friends with benefits." Evolving a somewhat novel variant to the exclusivist model, these individuals continued to date several others indefinitely without making significant restrictive commitments to anyone; for some, this pattern became a more-or-less permanent and preferred lifestyle.

For couples, the end of the last millennium saw the beginnings of an upsurge of interest in exploring ways in which the partners may be consensually more receptive to sexual/romantic engagements with others without sacrificing their primary relationship. By the end of the first decade of this century, the prevalence of involvement in such non-traditional relationship arrangements such as open marriages, polyamory, and three-(or more)somes had reached a level of popularity that it now may be regarded as a new counterculture.

Agreements

"Harmony is pure love,
For love is complete agreement."[19]

—Lope de Vega

Every couple has some kind of agreement that defines their relationship. In fact, it could be argued that if there were no agreement, there wouldn't be a couple, just two individuals, each doing whatever he or she wanted with no regard for the other.

Relationship agreements may vary greatly in terms of their explicitness. For many traditional couples, the shared understandings are implicit and never really discussed. Others may have codified their agreements into some kind of written form or extensively debated and negotiated verbal contract.

Marriage vows illustrate one form of traditional relationship agreement. Each party promises to "have and to hold," etc. (Interestingly though, it is only in the bride's version of the standard vows that the requirement to "honor and obey" is used.)

Exclusivity concepts are embedded into traditional wedding vows with such phrases as "promise to be true" and the old language, "To thee I plight my troth." ("Honey, have you seen my troth lately? I can't seem to find it anywhere.")

Relationship agreements may, of course, involve many aspects of the relationship, such as the sharing of resources, household duties, and so on. Agreements regarding the sexual/loving aspects of the relationship may be viewed as varying along a continuum expressing the degree of freedom to relate to outsiders.

At one extreme, the most restrictive agreements prohibit one or both partners from even the appearance of any contact with others of the opposite gender. (Think of the Muslim woman in her burqa who may be severely punished for even making eye contact with an adult male other than her father or husband.)

At the other end of the continuum, some contemporary couples have negotiated mutually consensual agreements allowing for each partner to explore and experience sex and/or love with outsiders while still maintaining a bonded relationship with each other.

In current Western society, most couples, married or not, would fall within the moderately restrictive range on the relationship agreement scale of sexual/loving behaviors with outsiders. Even most traditional couples usually agree that, for each partner, some leeway in erotic/romantic actions may be permissible.

Dancing with others, dressing a bit provocatively, and light flirting may often be considered acceptable within the bounds of a traditional or exclusive relationship. For most mutually-possessive couples, however, a rather firm line is drawn prohibiting sexual touching or expressing of emotional intimacy to outsiders.

The partners in a possessive couple are usually acutely aware of what is and what isn't permissible and are cognizant that to cross this line may result in significant relationship consequences. Accusations of intimacy violations with outsiders make up a very significant percentage of the conflicts seen in monogamous couples.

The traditional sexual/romantic boundaries may vary somewhat from couple to couple but are remarkably consistent across the vast majority of couples in our culture. So much so that transgressions are easily perceived as such by all and become common fodder for Country/Western song lyrics (for example, "My wife ran off with my best friend, and I miss him.")

Children, teenagers, and young adults are socialized into this value set by authority figures and the entertainment industry. As a result, few people question whether the exclusivist model of sexual/loving relationships is the best, or even the only, alternative. For almost everyone, it is simply a cultural given.

The implicit message is: "This is the way we do things in our society. Your goal is to search for and find your one true love, get married to that person, and live happily ever after, being completely faithful to your one and only spouse. Woe to you if you do not comply."

For most people, complying with the directives of the exclusivity model just seems like the natural and right thing to do. It's especially easy when one is newly in love. It's usually when the relationship matures that problems become apparent in the traditional, possessive relationship style.

As a relationship becomes inevitably less intense over time, the partners in a couple are often faced with difficult decisions involving the complexities of love, lust, honesty, trust, and so on. Continuing to bind oneself to a fidelity commitment may no longer seem like the most rational course of action.

As intensity fades, many couples seek professional assistance to attempt to rekindle the flame of their former relationship. Weekend workshops, promising renewal of passion between the partners, are a booming business. Like weight-loss fads, however, there is little evidence that these experiences have any lasting effect.

Couples may enter some form of marriage counseling as an attempt to bolster flagging interest in the erotic aspects of the relationship. Although couples' therapy can, indeed, be helpful in assisting many partners to achieve a more adaptive union with each other, there is again little evidence that it has any direct effect on increasing passion.

For most traditionalists, it looks like a black or white situation—i.e., either be faithful or stray. For them, abandoning sexual or romantic fidelity to one's partner means betraying the relationship. For these individuals, if (or more likely, when) passion for their one-and-only fades, no other sex or love partners are ethically permissible.

Individual responses to this universal dilemma generally involve the sacrifice of something or someone. Most people either suppress their need for passion or betray the trust of their partner by having a covert affair or abandon the relationship and search for a new love/sex partner. Usually, none of these alternatives result in happy outcomes for those involved, and instead, often create significant suffering for all (except the attorneys who profit from this dilemma).

CHAPTER TWO

Non-Exclusive Arrangements

Some couples are now negotiating agreements that involve the freedom to explore sexual and/or romantic activities with others but only within the context of a commitment to maintain their own relationship as primary, although not exclusive. These new relationship agreements can take many forms and may be quite fluid, changing with the evolving needs and desires of the partners.

Instead of following the standard trajectory, these adventuresome couples are choosing a different path. The choice to incorporate some type of non-exclusiveness into their relationship is a significant existential decision for these couples. It opens some new options and closes others with quite complex results and an unpredictable cost/benefit ratio.

Couples interested in moving toward a more non-possessive form of their relationship may or may not consciously consider, or even be aware of, the pros and cons of this alternative. In addition, they may not be fully cognizant of what obstacles they may face in implementing the shift toward non-exclusivity.

The traditional relationship model is so pervasive in our culture and language that we do not even have appropriate direct words to describe alternatives. As a result, we are left with having to use negative terms, such as non-possessive, non-monogamous, etc., which express what these relationships are *not* rather than what they *are*.

Terms like "free" or "independent" relationships do not seem to capture the essence of the concept for most people. The older term "open relationship" may be the closest expression that defines these alternative arrangement styles in a positive way.

"Open" contrasts nicely with the sense that most traditional relationships are closed to intimate involvement by others. "Open" further implies that the agreement forming the basis for the relationship is not fixed but is open to new possibilities.

The term "open" has many sexual connotations also. As in, "His arms were open to all as lovers" or "Although in her mind she knew she should be reserved in interacting with new people, she preferred a more open style of relating to attractive strangers."

The terms "open," "non-possessive," and "non-exclusive" can be used somewhat interchangeably but there are connotative differences among their meanings. Some relationships can be non-exclusive but quite possessive (such as a pimp and his prostitute), whereas other relationships may be non-possessive but are not open to outsiders (a group marriage, for example).

The Fourth Option

"Instead of thinking outside the box, get rid of the box."[1]

—Deepak Chopra

The fact that so many traditional relationships end up facing the unhappy choices of suppression, betrayal, or abandonment is old news. Couples have been struggling with how to cope with external desire at least since Eve bit into that apple.

What's new is the emergence over the last few decades of a couple-based solution to this conundrum. Some couples have been exploring together what might be considered a fourth alternative. In this option, the couple may choose to maintain their relationship, along with its foundation of trust, honesty, and shared values but agree conjointly to allow both partners to have some degree of erotic/romantic involvement with others, within the context of negotiated boundaries and limits.

Whereas the classic three alternatives (suppress, cheat, or breakup) typically create distressful outcomes, this fourth path seems to offer a win-win scenario for many couples. While the decision-making that results in the traditional outcomes is typically individualistic and is often driven by the desires of one of the partners more than the other, the negotiated settlement alternative is a consensual solution and one that is usually based on mutual respect and honest communication.

The recent rapid growth in popularity of this fourth option for couples is testament to its image as an attractive and effective solution to the existential issues faced by couples when love/passion are perceived as fading with time. However, as with the cautions we are familiar with on our commercial purchases, caveats may apply here also, such as, "Some assembly required" and "Positive results are not guaranteed."

For some couples, transitioning to a less possessive form of their relationship works well for them, and it may be seen in retrospect as a relationship-saving move. Other couples try the less traditional option, discover it's not for them, and revert back to the three basic choices. For some couples, the decision to explore non-possessive intimate arrangements leads directly to the dissolution of their relationship.

For the partners of some couples, a somewhat unexpected positive outcome of the decision to go non-possessive is the rekindling of physical and emotional intimacy between themselves. For example, some spouses, who have not had satisfying sex with each other for a long while, may find that the experience or even the possibility of having sex with others re-energizes their own passion for each other.

A husband may say, "Now that she is dressing more provocatively and flirting to attract more interest from other men, I find my wife sexier." She may say, "Now that he is free to be more charming and seductive towards other women, I find my husband sexier too."

A related fringe benefit of the non-possessive option is the opportunity the partners may have to experience and learn new erotic and romantic skills. For many long-term couples, relationship boredom may be a result of routinized ways of engaging with each other.

Novel experiences with new lovers can open up whole new ways of sharing sexual and emotional intimacies that the partners can adapt to their own interactions. This script might unfold especially for couples who married young and who did not have a lot of prior sexual/loving experience with others.

So, in this alternate universe, a typical relationship trajectory would be one in which the partners start out completely monogamous and then, after some diminishing of intensity, morph their union into a non-exclusive version, still maintaining the best aspects of their original pair bonding.

Other individuals may come into a coupled relationship from a background involving a lot of sexual/romantic experience with many others. These individuals, although wanting to enter into a bonded/committed relationship with just one partner, may still want to structure it in such a way as to maintain the essence of their previous lifestyle. They may create a couple that is non-possessive from the start and they may never have had a monogamous phase in the arc of their relationship.

Whatever the form of their trajectory, couples choosing the non-possessive form of intimate relationships are simply trying to combine the best elements of being committed with the best aspects of being single. (She: "Are you married?" He: "Sometimes.")

Existential Decisions

"Two roads diverged in a wood, and I—
I took the one less travelled by
And that has made all the difference."[2]

—Robert Frost

Almost all people are motivated to establish and maintain their intimate relationships as possessive. In addition to cultural programming, there appear to be strong emotional (and perhaps biological) factors prompting the adoption of the closed form of relating intimately to another person.

The loving relationship may be so essential to one or both of the partners that it may be defined as the most important thing in their lives. The threat of loss of such a critical thing may create intolerable anxiety on the part of one or both of the partners. By attempting to possess the loved person, the possessor attempts to protect against the catastrophic loss of the relationship.

The biggest risk generally seen is the possibility that the loved person may abandon the current relationship and establish a new one with somebody else. By prohibiting or limiting the loved one's contact or type of involvement with others, the lover is engaging in a form of risk management.

In longer-term relationships, the threat to couples posed by outsiders is magnified because often, the stimulus prompting the exploration of extra-curricular activities is a sense of dissatisfaction with at least some aspects of the current relationship. Someone new may look especially attractive, especially in comparison to the often overly-familiar characteristics of one's long-time partner.

When two people first come together in a loving alliance, the perceived quality of their interaction is often very high. Over time, almost invariably, intensity diminishes and one or both of the partners may find themselves drawn towards ways to re-experience intense romantic/sexual feelings again.

In a situation where Eve no longer feels the passion she once felt with Adam, she may want to explore external possibilities to reignite her arousal. In this scenario, Adam is faced with a difficult choice, if he wants to maintain the relationship. Essentially, his only two options are:

1. Attempt to enforce a taboo on Eve's roaming, or,
2. Suggest/agree to a non-possessive form of their relationship.

Each of these alternatives has somewhat predictable positive and negative consequences.

If Adam opts to maintain unshared possession of Eve, he may be successful in preserving his relationship with her. His success may be due primarily, or at least largely, to the restriction of opportunities for Eve to develop any competitive relationships.

Adam's success may come at a price, however:

- Eve may feel resentful at being restricted and at not being allowed to seek gratification for her strongly-felt needs.
- Eve may view Adam more negatively—for example, not only is he unable to stimulate her as much erotically or romantically any more, but now he is also becoming controlling and possibly punitive.
- Eve may act in defiance and develop outside hook-ups covertly (with some snake!), creating a potential breach of trust in the primary relationship.

If Adam chooses instead to allow Eve the freedom to engage in external liaisons, whether sexual, romantic, or both, again consequences are likely. Among the positives are the following:

- Eve may feel more positively toward Adam for his recognition and validation of her needs for stimulation, arousal, and satisfaction.
- Eve may find one or more outside lovers with whom she can get these needs met and will feel more satisfied and happier as a result.
- Eve will have minimal need to engage in covert affairs that could result in a trust violation.
- Adam and Eve will be more able to maintain openness and honesty in their communication.
- Adam may negotiate with Eve a similar arrangement for himself and be able to enjoy benefits similar to what she is experiencing.

Adam's decision to allow Eve relationship freedom may, however, result in some negative outcomes:

- If Eve takes up with a new lover whom she finds significantly more satisfying than Adam, and Adam becomes aware of this, Adam may have to cope with feelings of reduced self-esteem and/or jealousy.
- Eve may be less available to Adam if she spends considerable time with external lovers.
- Eve may be influenced by external lovers to modify her shared values with Adam.

- Eve may find someone else who may want to take her away from Adam and not be willing to share her with him.
- Both Adam and Eve may have to guard their non-possessive relationship against disapproval from others who may have more traditional values. ("Yes, God, we were just talking about it.")

In a non-possessive relationship, each partner is willing to share the other, at least in some ways, with outsiders and allow the other partner to develop sexual and/or romantic connections with those outsiders. If the outsiders are also willing to share, then the threat regarding the loss of the shared partner is greatly reduced (but not eliminated entirely).

The most feared outcome is that if a partner is given freedom to engage in relations with others, that partner may hook up with someone who does not want to share and that the shared partner may be so enamored by this new lover that s(he) may abandon the current partner and establish an exclusive relationship with the former outsider as a new partner. This is not a trivial threat because new lovers most often come with an enhanced aura of desirability, at least at first.

If Jennifer lets Brad roam, Brad may find Angelina more desirable/exciting than Jen. If Angelina is not willing to share Brad, Jen may find herself alone as Brad separates from her to form a possessive relationship with Angelina. This outcome results in multiple negatives for Jen. Not only has she lost her primary partner but her self-esteem and status may suffer losses also. (For celebrities, at least, there may be some compensatory positives, however, in terms of career-enhancing media exposure.)

Advantages, Disadvantages, and Barriers

"We always deceive ourselves twice about the people we love—first to their advantage, then to their disadvantage."[3]

—Albert Camus

To their adherents, non-possessive intimate relationships offer the possibility of many positive outcomes. Compared to traditional, exclusive relationships, those benefits most often identified with the non-possessive alternatives include the following:

- Sexual and/or romantic desires can be expressed and explored openly and do not need to be suppressed.
- Dysphoric emotions, such as anger, guilt, and jealousy, can be minimized and skills learned to control them.

- Abusive behaviors, such as controlling, punishing, and aggression toward others, can be greatly reduced.

- Excitement, arousal, and satisfaction can be experienced via extra-couple intimate activities.

- Intimacy between the primary relationship partners can be enhanced through the sharing of the anticipation, observation, and/or description of external sexual adventures.

- Honesty, trust, and mutual support between the relationship partners can be enhanced through the development of clear and assertive communication skills.

- New friends with similar values can be found, and these friendships can be enduring.

Only some individuals and couples are able to incorporate a degree of non-possessiveness into their intimate relationships, however. Those who have tried and have had negative experiences identify the following downsides:

- External intimate activities may be so seductive to one partner that (s)he may act to terminate the primary relationship.

- A certain quality of innocence may be perceived as lost or diminished when outsiders are granted intimacy privileges that were once exclusive to the primary partners.

- Other people with more traditional values may regard the non-possessive couple negatively.

- For some people, external intimate activities, even though consensual, may be a violation of their ethical, moral, or religious values.

- For married couples, "adultery" may be considered a violation of local laws and may place them at risk for civil or criminal sanctions.

- Increased contacts with multiple partners may increase the risk of sexually transmitted infections (STIs).

Obstacles must be overcome before a couple can achieve success in transitioning to a less possessive form of their relationship. Couples attempting to make this transition point to the following barriers to becoming less exclusive:

- Redefining a relationship as non-possessive requires reconstituting the bonding agreement between the partners to be more fluid and less fixed and the nature of the relationship itself to be more voluntary and less mandatory.

- Most individuals need to reach a level of maturity and self-confidence before they can cope successfully with a non-possessive intimate relationship.

- Most intimate relationships need to progress to a level of stability, and one in which both partners are committed to sustain, before a transition to a more open form will be successful.

- Moving to a non-possessive relationship requires the partners to be comfortable with an alternative lifestyle that is significantly at odds with traditional values.

- Giving up some sexual and/or romantic exclusiveness to one's partner in an intimate relationship may require a significant adjustment in the couple's relationships with family members and friends.

- Because almost all religions strongly prohibit sexual activities outside of sanctioned relationships, couples who are involved in their faith may need to reconcile their activities with these prohibitions.

Couples that explore non-possessive alternatives to their relationship typically find that they must carefully weigh the costs and benefits of this existential shift. In addition, they must consider whether or not they have the personal resources and the determination to overcome the many challenges they will encounter in making this lifestyle change.

Couples exploring extracurricular involvements may also find themselves influenced by the so-called "Coolidge effect." This term, coined by animal mating behavior researchers,[4] has been used to refer to the commonly observed phenomenon of heightened display of interest in new sexual partners even when little interest is shown toward a current partner.

Legend has it that the former U.S. president Calvin Coolidge and his wife were separately being shown around a farm and Mrs. Coolidge noted that the sole rooster was mating very frequently. "Point that out to Mr. Coolidge," she said to her guide. When Calvin was told, he noted that the rooster was mating with a different hen each time. "Point *that* out to Mrs. Coolidge," he said.

Defining Terms

"'The question is,' said Alice, 'whether you can make words mean so many different things.'"[5]

—Lewis Carroll

Some of the clearest indicators of the status of any concept are the words and terms used to describe and define it. Concepts that are well accepted in a culture tend to have descriptive terms that are simple and direct (for example, *War and Peace*). More marginalized notions, or those that are less well incorporated into a society's mores, tend to have descriptors that are less straightforward.

So it is when people have attempted to describe and define the many variations of intimate relationships that are non-traditional, i.e., different from the one man and one woman united in matrimony, FAOTDDUP (forsaking all others, 'til death do us part).

The standard model for intimate relationships is described and defined by many terms, almost all of which are direct and positive, i.e., "monogamous," "traditional," "fidelity," and so on. When we try to talk about alternative types of intimate relationships, especially those not based on sexual or romantic exclusiveness, we find it difficult to come up with straightforward words and terms to describe these arrangements.

So we are left with words and terms which convey what these relationships are *not*, like "non-traditional," "non-monogamous," "non-possessive," etc. Alternative models of intimate relationships still do not have direct and affirming terms to define them or even any well-accepted words to describe them. Although these kinds of non-standard intimate relationships have apparently been around almost continuously in human (and animal) history, there have been surprisingly few successful attempts to describe them directly without resorting to negations.

Part of the descriptive difficulty stems from the wide variety of alternative intimate relationships, each somewhat different from the others. So far, it appears that no one has coined a term that describes them all as a group of alternatives. It may be that the only thing they have in common is that they are all different from the standard model.

The term "open" has gained some currency in describing both an attitude and a range of intimate relationships that are not of the traditional variety. But not all alternative intimate relationship formats are open, however. Many threesomes, group marriages, etc., are closed to outsiders, for example. In this way, they are structurally similar to the traditional monogamous arrangement; they just involve more than two partners.

The use of the term "poly" has also achieved some acceptance, especially in contrast to the "mono" prefix. Thus, we may contrast polygamous (literally, many unions) with those that are monogamous. But few people involved in the spectrum of contemporary alternative intimate relationships would describe their arrangement as a type of polygamy, primarily because of the very negative connotations of this term due to its religious and patriarchal associations.

The term "polyamorous" is an example of a relatively new word which was coined to describe those involved in multiple concurrent intimate relationships; this term has been adopted broadly to refer to adherents of this particular lifestyle. Interestingly, there is no contrasting form of this term that is in common use to refer to those who choose to be involved in intimate relations with only one other at a time. (Shall we describe those who love only one at a time as "monoamorous"?)

The definition of the term "poly," which from the Greek means "many," also limits the use of this prefix, as it wouldn't apply in situations where maybe only one or two more are desired. ("Let's not get greedy here," said Polly.)

Also from the Greek, "gamous" implies marriage or at least a bonding together, and this suffix is problematic in describing those intimate relationships that are not legally bound and/or are more fluid.

So, overall, there do not appear to be many (if any) words that can be used to refer to the full range of alternative intimate relationships and especially few that are direct, i.e., that describe what they are rather than what they are not.

The one thread that seems to run through all of the alternatives to the traditional model is the elimination of, or at least some reduction of, a sense of possessiveness. The partners involved in all these arrangements have in common the willingness to give up some element of control over each other's thoughts, feelings, and actions.

So where does "love" fit into all this? Not all loving relationships involve sex, of course, and certainly not all sexual relationships involve loving. So, although love and sex frequently go together, clearly these two can exist independently in relationships.

Some couples describe their transition into non-possessiveness as a sort of divorce. Instead of divorcing each other, however, they agreed to divorce love from sex, keeping the former for themselves and outsourcing the latter.

"Intimacy" implies personal closeness, thorough familiarity and special interactions not granted to others. The term "intimate relationships" can thus be used to refer to those that are physically intimate (sexual) or emotionally intimate (loving) or both.

The "commitment" in a committed relationship is the pledge to abide by the agreement that defines the relationship. "I won't have sex with anybody but you" is the standard clause in almost all monogamous unions. It's not so much that the partners are committing themselves to each other; it's more that each is promising to not violate their relationship agreement, whatever that may be.

"Exclusive" generally implies one-and-only, excluding others, solely with you, and so on. Exclusive intimate relationships generally involve an agreement that prohibits the partners from engaging in behavior with outsiders that may be construed as erotic or romantic.

"Romantic" relationships are those that involve attempts at courtship, seduction, and idealized perceptions of the loved one. Romance usually involves sex but not necessarily. (Read Plato.)

Whereas "possession" may be a necessary condition to allow for exclusivity, possession does not necessarily require exclusiveness.

A man may have a possessive relationship with a condo unit he owns but, at times, may loan it out for use overnight by a friend or even rent it out to visitors on weekends and still maintain his possessive relationship with the unit. If he did the same with his wife (!), however, he could still claim he had a possessive relationship with her but it would just be non-exclusive.

CHAPTER THREE

Non-Possessive Relationship Issues

Behavior is the final common pathway, incorporating, sifting, and balancing all "upstream" elements. What we ultimately do is almost entirely directed by what we think and what we feel. Our cognition and our emotions are in turn influenced by our genetics/neurophysiology, our individual learned experience, and by the social programming of our culture.

Anyone involved in any kind of intimate arrangement must deal with many complex issues and must cope with varied influences, both internal and external. Those who adopt a non-possessive relationship style, however, seem to manage these universal challenges in ways that are significantly different from those who maintain a more traditional form of their union.

Mate Guarding

As Shakira sings, "Underneath your clothes . . . that's *my* territory,"[1] it reminds us of how most people guard their lovers' bodies against encroachment by potential competitors.

Possessiveness is pervasive. The traditional viewpoint (that loving relationships must be monogamous) is the commandment not only in our society but across virtually all cultures. The few examples of societally-approved non-possessive arrangements (which only occur in non-Western societies) are so highly unusual as to excite widespread attention, even if they might not be entirely true. (See the controversy regarding Margaret Mead's *Coming of Age in Samoa*.[2])

The fact that non-possessive relationships were found by the early anthropologists only in some "primitive" cultures was taken by the current moral authorities as proof that these types of arrangements existed only because these societies were so uncivilized. (See Bronislaw Malinowski's *The Sexual Life of Savages.*[3])

In the view of most social theorists, theologians, and others, modern Western civilization had clearly evolved to the more advanced level of insistence on the one-man, one-woman principle. A stronger version of this argument is that we became more civilized precisely because of the prohibition against multi-partner intimacies. (See Wilhelm Reich's *The Invasion of Compulsory Sex Morality.*[4])

Historically, the excluding of outsiders from participating in intimate relationships has apparently been the norm since people first started forming bonds. As far as is known from written records, there have been no historical eras, at least in Western civilization, in which the sharing of one's intimate partner was a widely accepted practice. On the contrary, guarding of one's mate against the encroachment by potential competitors has been the almost universal standard operating procedure.

This territorial imperative has motivated creative works in literature, drama, music, art, etc., which have focused on the commonly-accepted need to protect one's personal relationship "property." Not too surprisingly, many of these well-known productions have portrayed the great personal tragedies resulting from obsessive mate guarding. (See *Othello*.)

The "(s)he is mine, don't touch" approach is so geographically and historically consistent as to elevate it to a sort of a wisdom-of-the-tribe status—i.e., so many people have believed in mate guarding for so long, it must not only be the right way but the only way. Few social theorists have thought to challenge this conventional understanding and possessiveness in intimate relationships has become accepted as the common sense.

The notion of possessive love is most likely an extension of the more fundamental property-rights concept. It's not much of a leap from considering myself to be the owner of a tool or an animal to feeling that I am the "owner" of my spouse. ("Yes," says the successful man, "I own a house, a car, and a wife.")

Clearly, there are gender differences in the expression of this imperative to possess and guard one's mate.

Being more physically and economically powerful, men have almost always tried to control most resources in their environment. It's no surprise, then, that men historically have attempted and succeeded (at least partly) in controlling women's intimate activities. Men have enforced their dominance through various "restraints" both psychological and physical (try Googling "chastity belt").

Perhaps being the greedier of the genders, men have also attempted to make multiple females their exclusive property through a wide variety of ownership-like arrangements, such as polygyny, harems, and so on. Truly polyandrous societies, in which one woman guards more than one man, are so rare that it is difficult to find any bona fide examples beyond the (mythical?) Amazons.

Mate guarding by men, if not more prevalent and intense, is at least more overt than its converse. In one of the great ironies of human relationships, if it were not for the well-known propensity of men to attempt to spread their seed as widely as possible, it would not be considered so necessary by men to guard their own mate so diligently. ("It must be a guy thing," said Dolly.)

Women guard their mates too, however, sometimes just as intensely. The ideals of "sisterhood" usually do not extend to sharing one's inamorato with other women.

Of course, women have also evolved methods of controlling their male partners, at least in terms of men's legendary roaming behavior. One of the most common strategies used by women is to barter sexual exclusivity rights to themselves in return for the voluntary adoption of the same restrictions by their men.

An argument can be made that the institution of marriage has been developed primarily for the benefit of women to give them a socially acceptable way to control the philandering activities of their men who would otherwise stray into new relationships.

Divorce law has also evolved to protect a woman's "investment" in her man. In most jurisdictions, it is primarily the husbands who are at risk of punitive sanctions if they are unfaithful to their wives. This threat is yet another way in which our society enforces pair bonding and discourages multi-partner arrangements.

In most countries' jurisprudence, the law recognizes not only the right, but also the obligation, to protect one's intimate relationship "property" from sexual or romantic "theft" by interlopers. One only has to consider the all-too-frequent case of the jealous husband shooting his wife's lover. In these scenarios, judges and juries usually grant some degree of leniency to the perpetrator based on the presumption of these "property" rights and duties.

For couples who have adopted a non-possessive style of relationship, mate guarding is generally not a significant imperative. When one grants one partner the freedom to engage intimately with others (subject to some limitations) there is obviously less need to guard against this happening.

Many couples who have transitioned to a non-exclusive arrangement report a sense of relief in being freed from the former mate-guarding mentality. With intense vigilance regarding their mate's activities no longer a major concern, the partners may find themselves freer to relax and enjoy themselves (and others) more.

Jealousy

"O! beware, my lord, of jealousy;
It is the green-ey'd monster which doth mock
The meat it feeds on."[5]

—Iago in Shakespeare's *Othello*

The affective state we call "jealousy" is usually felt as some combination of the more fundamental emotions of anxiety and anger. It typically arises when an external threat is perceived to some aspect of an intimate relationship. Generally, the more possessive the relationship, the more acutely the jealous reaction is felt.

Couples who are attempting to transition their relationship to a less possessive form may find that feelings of jealousy emerge without warning and are difficult to cope with. For example, even though both partners may have agreed in advance that it would be permissible, the first time a husband sees or hears of his wife having intimate contact with another man, he may experience an unexpected visit from the "green-eyed monster."

The potential for loss of one's possessions of any kind to a competitor appears to be such a fundamental human fear that it may be hard-wired into our neural/cognitive structures as part of our evolution from the early primates. The things we own (property, resources, etc.) can sustain us and the need to protect them from theft by others is probably rooted in our biology.

This territorial imperative is seen, of course, in many species of animals that "jealously" guard their mates. Nevertheless, there is compelling evidence to support the existence of non-possessive sexual behavior in many other species, even in those that were previously thought to be completely monogamous. (Read *Sex at Dawn*[6] for a fascinating review of the evidence.)

[*Disclaimer*: I know what some of you guys may be thinking, but in the spirit of full disclosure, I regret to inform you, dear reader, that the above book has absolutely nothing to do with your early-morning erection.]

Gender differences are common in the experience of jealousy. Men, typically, are more likely to feel a jealous reaction when they perceive an external threat to the sexual exclusiveness of "their" woman. Women are more likely to experience jealousy regarding potential threats to the emotional exclusiveness of "their" man.

Because "swinging" usually involves sex with minimal emotional attachment, it may be easier for a woman to adjust to but harder for a man to cope with. Polyamory, which usually involves a significant romantic component, may be the reverse.

Some non-possessive adherents establish a goal of being jealousy-free in their intimate relationships. Such personal-growth objectives can be found especially in polyamorous and other multi-partner communities. Skeptics, however, claim that the absence of jealousy may just mean the absence of caring enough about any one person.

An extension of this perspective is commonly found among some possessive people who actually value jealousy as an indicator of sufficient strength of the emotional bonding on the part of their partner. Many women, in particular, are skeptical of the commitment of a man who does not react emotionally when attention is paid to his partner by other men. ("Doesn't he love me enough to at least get jealous?")

How do couples who are exploring the transition to non-possessive intimate relationships manage feelings of jealousy? Successful strategies appear to involve education, communication, and agreements.

Knowing what to expect is most often helpful in managing emotional reactions. Some recreational-sex clubs, for example, offer "newbies" the opportunity to attend events, such as lectures, workshops, and so on, which provide practical information about the range of activities and feelings that tend to occur in extra-partner encounters. At some venues, attendance at these training sessions is mandatory to gain admittance to the club.

Most couples find that jealousy can be limited (but not completely eliminated) by establishing a clear agreement regarding boundaries. Negotiating a consensus upfront specifying what is and what is not acceptable seems to be beneficial to most couples trying to manage jealous feelings.

Honest communication between the partners regarding feelings of anxiety, anger, loss, and more can at least allow each to gauge the extent of potential reactions. A frank discussion of what-ifs and possible scenarios can avoid traumatic surprises.

Those who are not assertive in identifying and communicating their true feelings to their partner seem to be the most at risk for negative reactions. Unstated assumptions appear to be the most common source of post-(extra)coital distress. ("But honey, I thought you wouldn't mind when I rode off with that motorcycle gang.")

Trust

"Love all, trust a few."[7]

—Shakespeare

Trust, in the context of a relationship, generally refers to the expectation on the part of each partner that the other partner will act as he/she has agreed to act and not act in ways that he/she has agreed not to act. Adhering to the agreement and respecting the boundaries agreed to is, of course, essential to maintaining trust in the relationship. Trust in one's partner is, in turn, the most effective counter to jealousy.

When one partner behaves in a manner not agreed to and the other partner learns of this transgression, that partner may feel hurt, angry, and betrayed. In a traditional, fidelity-based relationship, this betrayal feeling most often occurs when one partner has extra-relationship sex.

In a more sexually permissive relationship, betrayal feelings can also occur, of course, especially regarding violations of the agreed-upon code of conduct. For couples involved in these non-possessive arrangements, however, transgressions may be more easily forgiven or atoned for than would be the case if the couples were more possessive. For those in a more traditional relationship, sexual infidelities are generally viewed as more serious/unforgivable.

From each partner's perspective, the vague internal state that we think of as trust can be reformulated in terms of behavioral probabilities. If one's partner has always kept his/her promises in the past, one can predict with a high degree of certainty that (s)he will keep them in the future. Thus, one can have trust in relating to one's partner but from this perspective, the trust lies not in the other person's trustworthiness but in the confidence one has in making this prediction.

Similarly, if one's partner has violated agreed-upon expectations historically, one's trust in that partner may be quite low, regardless of whether that trust is viewed as an externally or internally-defined concept.

In most relationships, the ups and downs of trust are very unequal. Coupled partners tend to build trust of each other incrementally, with each agreement that is upheld adding a bit more to the accretion of confidence in the other.

Conversely, one single violation can wipe out a long accumulation of positive trust experiences. This is especially the situation with possessive couples in which one partner strays into a covert affair that is revealed. This transgression may never be forgotten, let alone forgiven, in spite of the fact that there may have been many prior years of fidelity.

Non-possessive couples, on the other hand, seem to view trust issues in a more forgiving and perhaps realistic way, taking human weaknesses and foibles more into account. To some extent, those involved in non-exclusive relationships appear to regard trust as more of a relative value rather than a moral absolute.

The perception that one's partner can be trusted to act in ways that are not harmful to oneself, however, may be the most important factor in maintaining a relationship of any kind. Conversely, betrayals of trust often present the most serious challenges to the continuation of any relationship.

In possessive couples struggling to reconcile after a covert affair by one of the partners, the aggrieved partner frequently complains that the external sex itself wasn't the biggest problem. It was the fact that their trusted partner concealed it and lied about it.

Notably, when one partner wants to terminate a relationship, they will often deliberately violate trust as a way to break the bonds of the partnership. (Watch a few episodes of *The Young and the Restless*.)

Honesty

"To live outside the law, you must be honest,"[8] writes Bob Dylan, reminding us that what is legal and what is honest may not always be the same thing.

When we say someone is honest, we generally mean that they ordinarily tell the truth, the whole truth, and nothing but the truth. Conversely, those who we regard as dishonest seem to be prone to tell us falsehoods, reveal only part of the story, or give us misinformation.

We typically understand that the purpose of dishonest statements is to deceive the listener into thinking that something is true when it is not or vice versa. Similarly, honest statements inform in a way that is accurate and are intended to enlighten the listener.

Honesty is thus a verbal concept; it resides in the telling about thoughts, feelings, or behaviors. More specifically, honesty is judged by the congruence between any one of these three aspects of human experience and the accuracy of how it is described.

Because thoughts and feelings are internal processes and thus not accessible to others, the only real way we have to judge honesty in another person is to observe how well that person's verbal description of their past behavior matches up with what we know about that actual behavior. If someone says, for example, "I did not have sexual relations with that woman," we may want to compare this statement with the semen stains on the (in)famous blue dress.

The partners of couples who adopt a non-possessive lifestyle generally place a high value on being truthful with each other. Although they may be deceptive in masking the nature of their relationship from a disapproving world, they are most often transparent and truthful in their communication with each other.

In general, the partners of non-possessive couples may be more honest with each other than those of their possessive counterparts. Most traditional couples, especially if they have been together for a long time, don't talk much about sex or romance anymore. Non-possessive couples engaging in these activities with outsiders, however, are forced to confront a host of intimacy and communication issues that they must deal with honestly if they are going to continue along this path successfully.

Achieving honesty regarding intimacies seems to have a generalizing effect. Many non-possessive couples report that once they discover that they can be fully truthful with each other regarding sexual behaviors, thoughts, and feelings involving outsiders, talking honestly about anything else is relatively easy.

With monogamous couples, the reverse is often the case. The partners in these unions often feel they must suppress, deny, or mask sexual thoughts about, feelings toward, and especially behavior involving outsiders. Not being truthful about sexual needs, desires, and actions often generalizes to being less honest about other aspects of the relationship.

Honesty in a relationship is most frequently tested when issues of disclosure arise. Telling your partner honestly what you thought, what you felt, and what you did is the essence of full disclosure. Disclosure can, of course, be about current thoughts, feelings, and future intentions also.

Similar to assertiveness, honest disclosure requires two components. First, you must identify your true thoughts and feelings (this is sometimes difficult) and recall accurately what your actions were. Then, you must convey these perceptions clearly to someone else in a manner they can understand. (This may not be easy either.)

Some couples have a history of not being truthful with each other. This less-than-fully honest style of communication between the partners will almost surely create problems for couples attempting to explore non-possessiveness in their relationship. The good news is that disclosure appears to be a learned skill and resources are available to help the honesty-challenged.[9]

Forthright disclosure of sexual activities can be fraught with anxiety reactions (for both partners) and is often a crucial "trust exercise" for couples newly experiencing intimacy with others. Again, the good news is that this interchange of frankness often gets easier with practice.

At the other end of the scale, more experienced and confident couples often learn to use honest disclosure creatively to prompt erotic arousal in their primary partner. ("I think your girlfriend is so hot and I would really like to do her sometime. That is, if you wouldn't mind, of course.")

Love

When Tina Turner sings, "What's love got to do with it,"[10] we understand that physical intimacy may not need to involve emotional intimacy.

There probably have been more attempts to define love than any other concept in the range of human experience. Poets, scientists, and everybody in between has weighed in on what it means to be in love. Still, we seem to have only a vague notion of what this elusive state of mind really is.

Almost everyone can recognize and identify the love experience, however. The disconnect between recognizing and defining love may be akin to the well-known comment by Supreme Court Justice Potter Stewart, who, presumably exasperated by the multiple attempts to pin down a legal definition of pornography, concluded that, "Although I am not able to define it exactly, I know it when I see it."[11]

Somewhere along the developmental trajectory of a coupled relationship, one or both of the partners may experience perceptions/feelings that they define as "love." A person who believes themselves to be in love customarily desires to maximize their contact/involvement with their love object. For most traditionalists, a corollary to this desire is the wish to limit the contact/involvement of their loved one with others, especially others who may be seen as competitors.

During a love affair, strong emotional states usually occur, including the bonding of sex and love and the use of sex to express feelings of love. To most traditional couples, the physical act of sex is the sine qua non of an intimate relationship. Because sex and emotional intimacy are synonymous for most monogamous couples, it is difficult for them to understand or accept how these could be separated.

In non-possessive relationships, however, the partners may agree to attempt to de-couple sex and love and explore the expression of each separately. In these non-traditional arrangements, the partners may be able to successfully separate sexual activity from emotional bonding or love.

A common (mis)perception among traditionalists is that if the two people in a couple are having sex with others, they must not really love each other. And yet, in many non-possessive relationships involving conjointly-approved sex with others, the primary partners may love each other as deeply as any monogamous partners do.

Because they have been able to disconnect erotic coupling from emotional intimacy, the partners in these non-possessive couples are able to engage sexually or even romantically with outsiders and still maintain deep emotional bonding with each other.

In a traditional relationship, the basic logic runs like this: "If you truly love me, you will want to have sex with me and only me." And conversely, "If you have, or want to have, sex with someone else then you don't really love me." Sexual exclusivity is thus most often seen as the litmus test of "true" love among monogamous people.

Sexual fidelity as an essential requirement of a romantic/conjugal union is, of course, deeply rooted in the religious and cultural values of most all societies. (Even in Oklahoma, love and marriage go together like a horse and carriage.)

In addition, sexual exclusiveness appears to be a strong need in most people that works psychologically, albeit in different ways, for both the lover and the loved one in most traditional relationships.

For those imposing restrictions, the fidelity demand is obviously one way of attempting to protect one's "territory" from external threats.

But why would anyone voluntarily agree to give up their intimacy freedom? One answer is that, for those accepting restrictions, fidelity commitments are a way to hedge against the possible anxiety-provoking temptations of external opportunities.

The mutual promise of sexual fidelity in a possessive relationship thus serves as a psychological defense mechanism for each partner, providing some protection against unacceptable/threatening impulses (for example, the urge to comply with an attractive outsider who may be proposing an encounter).

To not have such a commitment to exclusivity would require each partner to make independent decisions, based on the merits of each case, and not rely on a blanket exclusion clause. ("No, of course I can't go out with you. I'm married!")

For some non-possessive partners, allowing each other to have erotic/romantic contact and involvement with outsiders is what defines them as more enlightened than most traditional couples whom they view as still entrapped in issues of control, restrictions, and ownership. In their opinion, to give one's partner freedom is the ultimate expression of true love.

Similar to passion, love episodes tend to have a trajectory in which the love experience builds initially, peaks at some point, and then declines in intensity. Whereas passion may fade away almost completely in a long-term relationship, initial romantic love may evolve into a less intense, but more stable, form of loving/caring in a more mature version of the relationship.

Typically, most people seek the upswing of the love rollercoaster, enjoy the zenith, and then, at some point on the decline, start questioning their commitment to stay on the current ride. The fresh insight of non-possessive couples is that you don't have to give up what you may still love in order to re-experience the rush of new love and/or passion.

As such, this non-possessive approach may offer a novel solution to the age-old question of how to keep love alive.

Intimacy

(A man comes up to Gracie, puts his arms around her, kisses her, and she kisses him back enthusiastically. After he leaves, she walks over to George.)

George: "Who was that!?"
Gracie: "I have no idea. I never saw him before."
George: "You didn't even ask his name!?"
Gracie: "My mother told me never to talk to strangers."[12]

—Burns and Allen

Our relationships with other people can be seen as existing along a continuum of allowed familiarity. With some persons, we maintain the utmost distance and keep all contacts on a very impersonal level. At the other end of the range, we may grant access to our most private thoughts, feelings, parts, and experiences to one or more lovers or confidants.

Generally, we maintain a degree of reserve with someone we have just met. As our experience with that person grows, we may allow increased familiarity. Non-possessive people are often adept at short-circuiting this social convention. Many, in the various non-exclusive lifestyles, may seek the somewhat paradoxical experience of becoming intimate with strangers.

A common belief is that physical and emotional intimacy are mutually reinforcing. The idea here is that one naturally, or perhaps inevitably, leads to the other. Therefore, if one allows one's love object to have intimate physical interaction with an outsider, one risks that that love object may develop affection for and emotional bonding with that other person.

Virtually everyone is aware of this potential risk to an existing relationship if one or both of the primary partners were to engage in physical intimacies with outsiders. Many individuals appear to be very sensitive to this type of threat and, as a result, adopt possessive values as a way to minimize this risk.

Non-possessive individuals appear to manage this threat somewhat differently, however. These individuals may adopt alternative attitudes and procedures as risk-management strategies.

A viewpoint commonly expressed among those involved in non-possessive relationships is that although sex may indeed, at times, lead to love, it doesn't necessarily need to. A corollary of this perspective is that if one takes precautions, one can greatly reduce, if not entirely eliminate, the threat of emotional attachments developing with potential competitors.

Non-possessive couples, for example, often evolve agreements regarding outside intimate activities that are specifically intended to reduce the risk of either of the partners developing any significant bonding with anyone else. Reflecting the spirit of honest communication, so often valued by non-possessive couples, a common agreement is that if one partner perceives that (s)he is starting to develop "feelings" for an external sex interest, that partner will disclose this perception to their primary partner and the couple will explore potential courses of action conjointly.

Most non-possessive individuals appear to be able to compartmentalize sexual activity and maintain a psychological boundary between sex and emotional engagement. For those people, sex is engaged in with others only at a purely physical level, with minimal affective involvement.

An example of this separation is what might be termed the "Lolita paradox." (Although Humbert's nymphet was enthusiastic about intercourse, she regarded kissing as distasteful.)

Similarly, among swing couples, it is sometimes considered too intimate to attempt to kiss on the mouth the new partner with whom you have just had sex! For many non-possessives, erotic activities with outsiders are conducted on an almost business-like basis with nothing "personal" involved.

Non-monogamous couples may engage in sex with others, for example, with no more emotional attachment to the others than would be the case if they were engaging in some other non-sexual activity, such as playing tennis. ("Mixed doubles, anyone?")

This ability to eliminate, or at least limit, emotional involvement with others does not necessarily mean that non-possessive individuals are unable to feel any emotional connection during sex under any circumstances. Instead, these individuals seem to be able to switch off and on the emotional component of sexual activity, at will. So, the wife in a non-monogamous marriage may say that she has sex with other men but she makes love with her husband.

Attachments

"Love is just lust with jealousy added."[13]

—Lars von Trier

Most mature people have had personal experience with physical intimacy leading to a new emotional connection, often at the expense of a current relationship. Even if they haven't had direct personal experience, this progression is portrayed ad infinitum in the popular media (for an example, read any "bodice ripper" novel).

In addition to honest communication and status reports regarding feelings, non-possessive couples may develop other, more situational strategies to reduce the risk of emotional attachments forming with external sex partners. One common method, for example, is to limit outside sexual activities to situations in which opportunities for ongoing contact are minimal or reduced greatly.

For example, opportunities are available at some recreational sex clubs for relatively anonymous sexual contact. In these places, couples may engage in sex with others in specialized "play" rooms, such as designated orgy spaces or dark rooms. In these settings, there is often little need or opportunity for verbal interaction.

Non-possessive couples may engage sexually with other couples or singles in a relatively impersonal way at a club or party and never see again those with whom they had sex. Gays, of course, have been active participants in this impersonal, bathhouse-type sex for decades. What's new is that some hetero couples have recently adopted this method to minimize opportunities for the development of emotional ties and to keep it "just sex."

As an alternate approach to limiting opportunities for the development of emotional attachments with outsiders, some non-possessive couples may agree to have extra-relationship sex only outside of their geographical home territory. They may, for example, schedule trips to locations other than where they live for the purpose of hooking up with others for sex. Some couples may only have sex with others when they travel and they may book frequent vacations to recreational sex resorts, cruises, etc., for this purpose.

The external playmates (of both genders) encountered on these excursions are generally not available in close proximity to the travelling couple's home. As a result, these situational strategies greatly limit, but do not entirely eliminate, the likelihood of an ongoing emotional attachment developing to an outsider.

Another common method to manage the sex-leading-to-emotional-intimacy connection is to agree to prohibit solo sessions with outsiders. Many non-possessive couples will only have sex with others when both members of the couple are present.

A couple may say, "We only play together," meaning that they will only have sex with another couple when all four parties are in the same room at the same time. This restriction on any one partner having sex alone with an outsider is clearly intended to reduce opportunities for the development of emotional intimacy between that partner and the outsider.

In spite of all the precautions that may be taken by non-possessive couples, intimate bonding with outsiders can and does occur. One partner of one couple may develop emotional/romantic ties to the opposite (or same) gender member of another couple as a result of both couples sharing of physical intimacies with each other.

Although this situation can be a stressor for those involved, non-possessive couples are often able to reduce at least some of any potential distress between and among themselves better than most monogamous couples would. In the most enlightened scenario, both partners of each couple may all meet together to explore everyone's feelings and decide among themselves how to proceed.

Rather than being an unwanted problem, emotional/romantic connections among people having sex together may, on the other hand, be a desired fringe benefit of those involved in some non-possessive lifestyles. For those of the polyamory orientation, for example, the goal of having multiple concurrent sexual partners is often to develop multiple concurrent love relationships.

Also, in the swing world, some non-possessive couples report that one or more other couples, whom they started out engaging with just for sex, have evolved over time to become their closest friends. In one not uncommon arrangement, two couples, although living separately, may consider themselves one bonded unit that shares all intimacies together, both romantic and erotic.

Freedom

Freedom may be "just another word for nothin' left to lose,"[14] according to Janis Joplin, but for many people, living without restrictions imposed by other people is the ultimate purpose in life.

We generally understand the concept of freedom to be the flip side of concepts like limitations, restrictions, and control. To be free is to be able to do what you want and with whomever you want to do it with.

If indeed, all relationships involve agreements, then these by definition, create contractual obligations. Can the partners in a relationship also have freedom? For most monogamous couples, intimate extra-partner interactions are most definitely not free, in any sense of that word. ("A judge who thinks he's funny/Gave her half my money."—*Making Whoopee*.[15])

For many people involved in non-possessive relationships, however, a primary value is that of being able to be free from the control of others. Not being limited by obligations of intimacy faithfulness to their partner allows a person to be spontaneous in choosing who they can engage with sexually and/or romantically.

A closely related concept is the willingness to accept that the other person with whom one is involved in a primary relationship should have this freedom also. Thus, those for whom these ideas are important may both give and receive, to and from a primary partner, the freedom to pursue intimate relations with outsiders.

The so-called "free-love" movement of the 1960s was a popularized expression of this concept. It was not, as was misrepresented by the media, that sex was freely given, indiscriminately, to anyone. Rather, those who adopted the free-love philosophy did not restrict their sexual/loving involvement with others simply because of commitments to be "true" to any one person.

A logical extension of this approach was to grant the same freedom to others; hence, those of the free-love generation did not demand fidelity agreements even from their long-term partners. In this era, there was a popular emphasis on being as free as possible, both in terms of your own activities and in encouraging others to be free of restrictions also. Portrayals of this perspective were common in the pop music of the time, such as the lyrics by David Crosby, et al., "If you can't be with the one you love, love the one you're with."[16]

This type of mutually-freeing relationship arrangement was typical in organizations, such as the Sexual Freedom League,[17] which was briefly popular on college campuses in the 1960s and 1970s. (This radical organization faded away, however, possibly because at its meetings, the ratio of men to women often exceeded 20 to 1.)

Those activists in the women's liberation movement were also vocal proponents of freedom (for women at least) from coercive relationships. Similarly, one of the original themes of the feminists was to expose and counter the domineering and controlling behavior of men.

Of all the aspects of a woman's behavior that men have traditionally tried to control, probably none has received more attention than a woman's sexual activities. In some cultures, for example, the imperative to suppress any expression of a woman's sexuality, however slight or indirect, has become literally a religious crusade.

In western countries, feminists have raged against the idea that a woman could be considered the possession of a man. If they did marry, however, even most feminists were willing to grant sexual and romantic exclusivity to their husband, following the traditional, possessive model.

These somewhat radical perspectives of sexual freedom and feminism faded from popularity during the neo-conservative decades of the 1980s and 1990s. More recently, however, we appear to be witnessing a resurgence of interest in relationships based on freedom from control by others.

Those in the non-possessive camp have essentially designed and beta-tested a new model of freedom in relationships. Rejecting the traditional approach that any intimate involvement with outsiders is verboten, these couples have parsed the notion of intimacy freedom into those types which are acceptable and those which are not.

Flying their freedom flag, non-possessive couples often view their more traditional counterparts as mired in a slavery-like arrangement. For these alternative relationship couples, the bonds that hold them together do not include sexual intimacy bondage (unless, of course, it's of the B&D variety).

Commitment

Listening to the double entendres in Chet Baker's lyric, "She was too good to be true"[18] prompts us to reflect on the frequently observed gap between expectation and reality in our experiences involving fidelity.

Possessive couples often use the term "committed" to refer to their relationship. She is committed to him and he is committed to her in the sense that they each pledge their loyalty to each other via an exclusivity agreement, whether explicit or tacit. In the traditional monogamous contract, this exclusivity is generally understood to apply to all forms of intimacy, specifically prohibiting sex and romance with others.

The commitment is the promise to be "true" to one's partner by refraining from engaging in behavior that might give others the same rights to physical and emotional intimacy that are currently held only by one's partner. Violations of this promise result in accusations that the wayward partner has been untrue, i.e., to their commitment.

Single men are often accused (especially by matrimonially-inclined women) of having a fear of commitment. Perhaps, in the spirit of generosity, single women may attempt to "cure" an eligible bachelor of this anxiety. Rather than a phobia, or irrational fear, however, this stance on the part of single men may be reconceptualized as a rational decision to avoid taking on obligations that would restrict the exploration of future opportunities.

Non-possessive couples handle issues of commitment differently. Among couples involved in the swinging subculture, for example, the primary partners most often have a strong sense of commitment to each other. Their bond just doesn't include sexual exclusiveness, however.

The partners in a non-possessive couple typically have a committed relationship based on their past history, currently shared values, and future expectations of remaining together. Among other things, commitment to them means being supportive of their partner's needs and this support extends to needs for external sexual adventures.

Those involved in non-possessive relationships tend to be committed to their primary partner just as strongly as those who are involved in more traditional relationships. In fact, an argument could be made that the commitment between the partners of a non-possessive couple might be even stronger than that generally seen between the partners in a possessive arrangement.

With a possessive relationship, the behavior of each partner is more closely controlled and, as a result, commitment is not tested as much under potentially tempting circumstances. By comparison, the partners in a non-possessive relationship are, at least at times, "off the leash" in terms of sexual activities.

These adventurous partners must learn to cope with commitment challenges that their more traditional counterparts never have to encounter. Consequently, with this type of "stress-testing," a stronger sense of being bonded to one's primary partner may evolve among those couples who are successful in the non-possessive lifestyle.

Essentially, successful non-possessive couples have found a way to keep the best aspects of commitment in their relationship and discard those aspects that they feel are unduly restrictive and unnecessary. In effect, they are saying to each other, "I am here for you now and I will be here for you in the future and this commitment doesn't depend on whatever you or I do sexually with other people."

Choices

"Would you tell me, please, which way I ought to go from here?"
"That depends a good deal on where you want to get to," said the Cat.[19]
—Lewis Carroll

Moment by moment, all through our lives, we make decisions about what actions to engage in and, to some extent, what thoughts to think and what feelings to feel. Most of our choices are relatively mundane and have little impact on our current or future situation. A few, however, are what we might call existential, in that they set us off on a new path. Looking back on these, we can see that they were turning points in our lives.

At some juncture, a couple that becomes interested in exploring a non-possessive form of their union may make a conscious choice to engage in sex and/or romantic activities with outsiders. This decision will most likely alter the future course of their relationship and how they relate to others. Virtually all couples who have transitioned from a monogamous to a non-monogamous style remember when they decided to do this and regard the decision as a significant change of direction for themselves individually and as a couple.

In a traditional relationship (meaning, the sort usually seen in a monogamous married couple), each partner commits to a pledge of sexual fidelity to the other partner. This commitment may be explicit, such as in wedding vows, or just an implicit understanding, as in a single person agreeing to "go steady" with someone. In either case, each partner chooses to forego the pursuit of non-primary-partner sexual or romantic interactions and does not initiate or accept invitations for sex or romance with outsiders.

This choice is entirely voluntary. Other than in a few ultra-conservative cultures, no one is coerced into being monogamous. In traditional relationships, the partners intentionally choose to give up seeking or responding to opportunities for extracurricular sex/romance.

This sacrifice may often be seen as fair for both parties—i.e., "I'll choose to give this up for you if you will choose to do the same for me." In this way, the decision can be viewed as balanced and reasonable. The fairness aspect of this decision is often cited by individuals first coming together as a couple.

Over time, however, the exclusivist choice may come to be perceived as more required than optional. For some people, the notion of sacrificing such an important thing as choice of sexual/romantic associates is equivalent to allowing someone else to control your behavior. For these people, the traded-off gain in fidelity from their partner may not seem like such a good bargain eventually.

For some people, especially those who have a strong need to control the behavior of others, the main purpose of demanding an exclusive relationship is to restrict the choice of activities of their partner. In many traditional relationships, it is relatively easy to see the dynamics of one partner attempting to control and restrict the other's options and that other partner feeling their choices and freedom to be unduly limited.

Often, the words used to describe these arrangements reflect possession concepts, either explicitly or implicitly. One partner regards the other partner as a possession and the other partner feels "owned" by the first partner. In this situation, one or both of the partners in the couple may be motivated to revisit their choice points regarding exclusivity.

If, or more likely when, a traditional couple reaches the stage of questioning their exclusivity choice, they then face the dilemma of what to do about it. Some decide to just grin and bear it, others decide to start having affairs, and some decide to give up on the whole relationship.

Non-possessive couples choose a fourth path. By agreeing together to permit some external frolicking, the partners may each regain the power to make their own erotic choices.

Possession

"An object in possession seldom retains the same charm that it had in pursuit."[20]

—Pliny the Younger

When we say we possess something, we generally mean we own it and it belongs to us and us only. Perhaps, as with a car or a house, we have a document of title verifying our ownership. For many traditional couples, a marriage certificate is like a title conferring possession of each spouse by the other.

Wanting to possess something of value seems like a fundamental human characteristic. Throughout history and across all cultures, people have felt a strong need to own the things they found desirable. Along with tangible goods, people can also be regarded as possessions, for example, slaves.

Control is inherent in the concept of ownership. We exercise power over others by limiting who uses our possessions and by restricting what uses our possessions are put to. If a person is regarded as a possession, it naturally follows that the behavior of that person can/should be controlled by the "owner" of that person.

In a traditional relationship, there is usually some sense of ownership of each partner by the other. The agreement to possess and be possessed is generally seen as the essential commitment necessary to begin a monogamous relationship.

Individual people who define themselves as unattached generally do not attempt to exert any ownership control over those with whom they have intimate relations. Similarly, an unattached individual ordinarily does not expect or accept from a sex partner or romantic encounter any restriction on her/his own freedom to engage erotically or romantically with others. Indeed, the freedom to "play the field" is often regarded as one of the main perks of the single lifestyle.

At times, two single people may decide to get "serious" with the customary expectation that they will form a relationship that is intended to be more lasting than temporary. Typically, to mark this change in the relationship, each will agree to forego sex or romance with others.

This agreement is often seen as the critical element in defining a committed relationship. As the two individuals commit to intimate exclusivity, they in effect each grant ownership control of their own sexuality to their new partner.

Except in some extreme cases, such as human trafficking and some ultra-conservative religious societies, possession is voluntary for both parties in a relationship. In a traditional intimate relationship, each partner wants to possess the other and each agrees to be possessed by their partner. If one of the persons involved does not want to play the possession game, there is no ownership relationship.

Even the language we use to describe monogamous bonding reflects the concept of possessiveness. "Will you be *mine*?" or, "I'm all *yours*." We speak of *giving* oneself to one's beloved, as one would in the transfer of ownership of a tangible object.

When one person believes that they have a possessive relationship with another person, certain expectations generally apply. If Svengali feels that Trilby is his alone, he will likely want to control the activities of his "property" and maybe even her thoughts and feelings.

Svengali's interest in having a possessive relationship is easily understood. But what about Trilby's motivation?

Trilby may find some satisfaction in being possessed. Either with full awareness or subconsciously, giving up control of herself to somebody else may meet deep-seated needs.

If, indeed, Trilby can achieve arousal and fulfillment in this way, then we have a symbiotic relationship in which both parties get their needs met. This is what we see in sadomasochistic or bondage and discipline arrangements in which complementary desires are met through power imbalances.

Rousseau popularized the notion that the human race was originally non-possessive in all ways during our nomadic hunter-gatherer phase.[21] In his view, it was only when agriculture was developed that the concept of private property was established. From this perspective, possession became the snake in the Garden of Eden, seducing mankind away from its "natural" tendency to share all things, including each other.

Modern-day non-possessive couples may be seen as operationalizing Rousseau's ideals of sharing. By rejecting sexual control in a relationship, these pioneering partners sometimes view themselves as a model for how we all can live together less possessively.

Loss

"I used to kiss her on the lips but it's all over now."[22]

—Anonymous

Possessing one's love object clearly has strong appeal. But why do we so often feel such an intense need to own and control the person we love?

For many people, the threat of loss of the loved one is the most powerful motivator prompting the possessive urge. If, for example, I do not allow my loved one to have intimate contact with anyone else, I may have less risk that (s)he will abandon me for someone else who (s)he may find more attractive, exciting, satisfying, etc.

Compared to the tangible assets that one owns, one's loved one may be perceived as the most valuable possession of all and thus, the most necessary to restrict and control. For some people, their "one and only" may be viewed literally as irreplaceable.

The threat of possible loss of the loved one may be seen as a potentially catastrophic outcome. This threat may be a source of great anxiety that, in turn, may prompt greater attempts to double down on control and restriction.

Especially for those people who may doubt their own self-worth, the possible loss of the loved one may trigger fears of being unable to acquire another loved-person relationship. Attempts to "lock in" a relationship with possessiveness may thus represent an anxiety management strategy.

Some people are able to develop loving relationships that are non-possessive, however. For these individuals, the idea that a loved one should be owned, restricted, or controlled in any way is rejected, either explicitly or tacitly.

These people often see an inherent conflict between loving someone and also trying to limit what that person thinks, feels, or does. These non-possessive lovers may adopt as a guiding principle some version of the common adage, "If you love something, set it free."

As contrasted with those in the love-as-ownership camp, non-possessive lovers appear to be less fearful regarding the possible loss of their loved one. These restriction-averse people may have a more secure self-image and may be more confident regarding their ability to acquire another love object should the current one depart. Non-possessive individuals may view themselves as more attractive to potential new lovers and less needful of any specific person with whom to maintain an intimate relationship.

At the far end of the traditional relationship trajectory, one or both of the partners may want to terminate their commitment. At this time, one of the most common statements expressing this desire is for one of the partners to have sex with an outsider. In this way, that individual is taking back control of their own sexual/romantic activities and rejecting the possessiveness of their partner.

Instead of throwing out the baby of eroticism with the bathwater of monogamy, successful non-possessive couples are able to achieve a negotiated settlement in which the best parts of the relationship are maintained and the others are outsourced. For this compromise to work, each partner must be able to give up some degree of control and reduce their anxieties regarding the potential loss of the relationship.

Freed from the actual bonds of possession, experienced non-possessive couples can play with the trappings and the symbols for erotic effect. For example, at costumed play parties, it is not uncommon to see leashes and collars being worn, by both genders, as the sex "pets" are paraded around by their owners. (Insert "doggie-style" comment of your own choosing here.)

Altruism

"If you love someone, set them free."[23]

—Peter Max

Ordinarily, we expect people to act in ways that are in their own best interests. In fact, the propensity to choose self-rewarding behaviors is likely hard-wired into our neurophysiology and is clearly essential for the survival of every organism.

The observation that, under some circumstances, people may apparently choose actions that primarily benefit another person is somewhat counterintuitive. At times, these behaviors may even result in some sacrifice or loss to the person engaging in these altruistic actions. Why would someone do that?

The answer given by many non-possessive couples is that unselfishness is a tangible way of demonstrating caring and love for one's partner. Certainly, all loving couples may show some altruism in their relationship but non-possessive couples frequently extend this "gift" to include sexual intimacies with others.

The shift from possessiveness to non-possessiveness, for example, in terms of a partner's sexuality, can be criticized as a change from caring to uncaring. Certainly, for some couples, this may be true. The relationship intensity may have cooled so much that one or both partners may feel that there is not much need to control the other's activities anymore.

Some critics of non-possessive relationships interpret the shift to more openness as always indicating a shift toward a decreased level of caring between the partners. ("Why would any husband who truly loved his wife voluntarily allow her to have sex with other men?")

This sentiment is often echoed by the partner who does not want to transition the relationship to include intimate involvement with outsiders. ("If you want to have sex with someone else, then you don't love me as much, or at all, anymore.")

The fact that we rarely see non-possessiveness in couples who are in the first blush of a new love supports this association between exclusivity and strength of caring.

A contrarian perspective, however, is that a non-possessive relationship can actually represent a higher degree of caring than that found in most possessive unions. The argument here is that allowing one's partner the freedom to engage intimately with others is an act of unselfish mindfulness regarding their needs above what might be one's own egocentric wishes. Permitting freedom for one's partner is thus seen as a transcendent form of caring that is based on the partner's welfare rather than in the selfishness of ownership and control.

Couples enjoying successful non-possessive relationships often view themselves as morally superior and ethically advanced in comparison to those with traditional "vanilla" relationships. (Read *The Ethical Slut*[24] for a humorous how-to guide to achieving such transcendence.)

This perspective contrasts sharply, of course, with that of mainstream society and especially with that of our culture's more socially conservative elements who view non-possessive relationships as dysfunctional and probably psychopathological. These critics usually expect couples engaging in non-possessive intimate activities to be burdened by shame, guilt, and other self-deprecating feelings, as a result of their "abnormal" behavior. They are often surprised to see how happy and well-adjusted so many of these couples are.

Being involved in a non-possessive intimate relationship can sometimes result in somewhat unexpected, and at times, surprising feelings. For example, when faced with the prospect of a partner's sexual activity with an outsider, the other partner may feel arousal, rather than (or in addition to) jealousy.

Another somewhat counterintuitive reaction is that of genuinely feeling happiness in the witnessing or hearing of one's partner's pleasure as a result of intimate activity with another person. A husband, for example, may experience a loving sense of joy in observing his wife having an orgasm brought on by a new lover.

This phenomenon, which has been called "compersion," would appear to be the opposite of jealousy. (For a detailed description of compersion and its use as a therapeutic method, see the excellent review *Polyamory in the 21ˢᵗ Century*.[25])

The partners in a couple who are able to feel this type of empathy and generosity toward each other often believe they have reached a more evolved or mature plane in their relationship. They may contrast themselves with more traditional couples whom they regard as still struggling with selfishness.

So, while on the surface it might appear that a giving partner is acting in ways that seem to be not in their own best interest, in fact, this partner may experience several types of positive reinforcement from these altruistic actions. Along with the benefits to the other partner who is the recipient of these gifts of caring, unselfish behaviors such as these, may create a truly win-win outcome for the non-possessive couple.

In contrast to a perhaps more narrow view of altruism, which may emphasize sacrificing something of oneself to benefit someone else, many non-possessive people focus on how giving to their loved one can bring the joy of generosity to themselves. They may describe their style as one of "enlightened altruism."

CHAPTER FOUR

Yin versus Yang

As we have seen, non-possessive intimate relationships can be contrasted with those of the possessive variety in terms of the psychological issues described in the preceding chapters.

Those couples and individuals who have made the transition to non-possessiveness often think of themselves as thinking, feeling, and acting differently now. They may contrast how they used to be with the way they have become in terms of how they understand their relationship, how they view ethical matters, how they differ from others, and how men adapt to this change differently from the way women do.

Cognitive Shifts

> *"Cogito ergo sum."*[1]
>
> —Descartes

Thoughts, feelings, and actions are all interrelated, of course. How you think strongly affects how you feel and what you do. One of the great insights of psychotherapy is that if you want to help a person change their emotional state or their behavior, the best way to do that is to help them change how they think.

At those times when psychotherapy is effective, therapists often note a kind of paradigm shift in the client's cognitive processes. Often this entails a transition to a more adaptive way of thinking about oneself or one's world view.

Many couples who have successfully negotiated the transition from an ownership-based to a less possessive relationship appear to have engaged in a kind of restructuring of how they think. Starting from a traditional, proprietary-love perspective, these couples have been able to reconceptualize some elements of their relationship, such as sexual exclusivity, from being essential to being optional.

This process is generally quite selective; only some aspects are apportioned out to be shared with outsiders. Other aspects of the relationship remain the exclusive domain of the couple.

Jealousy is managed somewhat by focusing on the strength of these remaining bonds. Each of the partners in such a couple may engage in self-talk (either silent or vocalized) to reinforce changed perspectives. ("He may be having sex with other women but it's only me that he really loves.")

For most people in our society, the physical intimacy of sex is the ultimate "gift" that one person can give to another as an expression of love. To think of voluntarily sharing this gift with others runs counter to much of our cultural conditioning.

Couples who move toward non-possessive arrangements appear to engage in a cognitive shift as a kind of risk management strategy regarding this issue. In this restructuring of their thinking, they may downplay the significance of sex and recharacterize it to a more impersonal status, such as play or recreation.

This downgrading of importance allows them to feel less stress/anxiety regarding their partner's erotic engagements with others. Thus, we may observe the bumper-sticker slogan offered by some in the non-possessive camp, i.e., "Relax, it's just sex."

If we conceptualize a continuum of attitudes about sex, this change represents a seismic shift away from the traditional pole that sex is a kind of sacred activity to be shared with one's one-and-only, *only*, and that sex is the sine qua non of singular commitment.

Many young people, especially girls, adopt this conservative perspective that sex is to be saved and granted only to a potential life-long partner, exclusively (Google "virginity pledges"). Of course, more reactionary individuals take an even more (missionary?) position that sex is only for procreation and not pleasure.

The sex-as-recreation perspective is a somewhat recent and more radical extension of the purpose-of-sex continuum toward the opposite extreme. Non-possessive couples who define sex as "play" are able to consider erotic activity as just a more intimate form of socializing, a sort of horizontal dancing, perhaps.

By equating sex with recreation, a non-possessive couple may be utilizing a kind of cognitive disconnection in which sexual activity is decoupled from love and emotional intimacy. Sex with others can then be compartmentalized and regarded as separate from the ties that bind the primary relationship together.

A partner in a non-possessive relationship can then experience few if any negative thoughts or feelings when their significant other has sex with outsiders. ("Each week, my wife has a night out with her girlfriends and another night out with her boyfriends. It's all good.")

The attitudinal adjustments of non-possessive couples can be exceedingly complex and diverse. Among the most commonly expressed variants is that of maintaining the erotic and emotional intimacy connection with one's primary partner but not with outside sex-mates. ("I have sex with other women but I make love with my wife.")

Disconnecting sex from the elements that form the bonds of a loving relationship can be somewhat challenging, especially because it is so counter to our cultural conditioning. Even more radical disconnections may be observed, however, in some variations of non-possessive arrangements in which emotional intimacy only with one's partner is also jettisoned as a necessary tie that binds.

In some non-possessive relationships, such as those seen in the polyamory communities, each partner may not only have sex with others but may be actively and intensely involved in additional loving partnerships with others. Here, the traditional notion of loving only one person at a time is replaced by concepts emphasizing the feasibility and benefits of engaging in multiple simultaneous loving relationships.

The often-expressed viewpoint in these poly relationships is that love for one does not necessarily preclude love for others. An equally common perspective is that love for others does not necessarily diminish love for any one. ("I love my husband but I also love my boyfriends and my freedom to love them too just increases my love for my husband.")

Morality versus Ethics

"Morality is not properly the doctrine of how we may make ourselves happy, but how we may make ourselves worthy of happiness."[2]
—Immanuel Kant

Whenever we concern ourselves with questions of right and wrong, good or bad, and so on, there is no lack of systems or people eager to tell us which is which. Philosophers who toil in the field of ethics confront quintessential questions such as, "Is morality just whatever society deems it to be at any given time or are there 'higher' moral values to which we could/should aspire?"

To many people, those who engage in non-exclusive intimacies appear to be violating generally accepted standards of conduct. So, are threesomes, polyamory, group marriages, and the like immoral?

Most knowledgeable theorists conclude that the specific moral values of any culture are, to a large extent, selected via a kind of popularity contest. What is deemed to be acceptable is what is approved by the (moral) majority. So, by this standard, non-possessive intimate activities are definitely discordant with conventional social customs.

A darker perspective is that moral values are selected, inculcated, and enforced by those in power for the primary purpose of maintaining that power. (Read any of the futuristic dystopias, such as *1984*,[3] *Brave New World*,[4] and others, or better yet, any of the critical descriptions of the history and strategy of the Catholic Church.[5])

People engaging in non-possessive relationships represent a kind of minority opinion in the court of public values. As with most other minority perspectives, non-exclusive adherents claim some protection against the "tyranny of the majority" and the right to hold and express their non-traditional beliefs.

Couples involved in non-exclusive intimate arrangements generally do not think of themselves as immoral and rarely are ever troubled by feelings of guilt that they have transgressed in some way. On the contrary, most couples involved in swinging and related behaviors feel morally superior to monogamous couples and believe they have reached a higher level of morality than those of the "vanilla" world.

By refocusing the morality issue in terms of ethics, these non-monogamous couples point to their emphasis on truthful disclosure, honest communication, and harm avoidance for all parties, as evidence of their ethical enlightenment.

Easy contrasts are made with the commonly observed cheating behavior of traditional couples and the destructive effects of suppression, deception, and abandonment. To the non-monogamous, these ethical negatives appear to be the unavoidable consequences of possessive relationships.

If anyone has any doubt regarding the prevalence and popularity of cheating and deception, one has only to regard the explosive growth of websites, which are specifically targeted at partners who want sex with somebody else, without their spouse knowing about it. The best known of these, *ashleymadison.com*, now boasts of having more than 37 million subscribers who buy into their trademarked headline, "Life is short. Have an affair."[6]

Non-possessive adherents disdain deception and, instead, emphasize honest disclosure to those with whom they are involved. The ethical principles adopted by those of the non-exclusive persuasion are elaborated upon in several sources. For a well-written overview from a counselor's perspective, read *Love in Abundance.*[7]

Non-possessive couples often see themselves as relationship radicals. Like most iconoclasts, they reject the conventional mores of mainstream society and dance instead to the beat of a different ethical drummer.

Standards of morality change over time, though. If socially accepted values were to evolve toward greater acceptance of non-possessive intimate relationships, then those who espouse these freedom-based arrangements could move closer to being part of mainstream culture.

For example, over the past few decades, there has been a tectonic shift in societal attitudes toward wide acceptance of homoerotic couples. (Rip Van Winkle would be astounded if he woke up today and saw the success of the gay marriage movement.) For the current time, however, non-possessive intimate unions still remain firmly in the closet.

Personal Qualities

> *"If a man does not keep pace with his companions, perhaps it is because he hears a different drummer."*[8]
>
> —Henry David Thoreau

Individual differences among people clearly affect how each person responds to common challenges in life, such as forming and managing intimate relationships. Some psychologists theorize that people may be divided into various personality types, each having similar distinctive qualities that set them apart from the other types.

Couples who are successful in managing non-possessive intimate relationships appear to be composed of partners who possess certain individual characteristics that allow them to maximize the benefits and minimize the risks involved. Conversely, partners who try and fail to introduce an element of non-possessiveness into their relationship seem to have somewhat different personality factors that limit their management of the risk/benefit ratio.

The successful personal qualities of non-possessive couples can be in the realm of relatively enduring attributes, such as high levels of self-confidence, social skills, and sensuality. Other of their individual characteristics may be more appropriately considered personal values, such as having a high regard for freedom, independence, and the seeking of new experiences.

Couples in less possessive relationships appear to value the right to choose what is best for the individual more so than those having more traditional arrangements in which "family values" may trump individual liberties. Although the bonding that makes them a couple is important to non-possessive couples, so is the freedom from restraint on their personal behavior.

Successful non-monogamous couples are able to navigate a balanced course between the demands of the relationship and their independence as individuals. This navigation generally translates into pursuing one's personal needs when and where possible but avoiding behaviors that would cause distress to their partner. A couple living together may agree, for example, that it would be OK for each of them to have sex with other people but that these activities should take place outside their home and neither should bring an external lover into their own conjugal bed.

Feelings of security appear to be an important prerequisite to initiating and managing successful non-possessive intimate relationships. For a couple to cope with the inevitable challenges that non-exclusiveness poses, each of the partners must feel secure in the relationship with the other. In addition, each partner must have a sense of security regarding their identity as an independent person.

Insecurities, often felt as doubts about one's partner or oneself, seem to predict failure if a couple attempts to open their relationship to intimate involvement with others. Given that relationship and individual insecurities are so prevalent, it might be speculated that this is a major reason why the vast majority of all couples remain monogamous.

Insecurity is usually experienced as feelings of inadequacy, low self-esteem, limited self-confidence, and so on. By comparison, feelings of security among successful non-possessive couples are often expressed along the lines of an "I'm OK, you're OK, we're OK, and our lovers are OK" kind of statement.

The sense of security felt by these sex-positive couples may be related to the observation that self-confident people have higher threat thresholds and do not feel a need to defend their possessions as intensely as those with lower ego strength.

Couples that feel good about their non-possessive intimate relationship often adopt an implicit risk management projection or worst-case scenario analysis that is fundamentally positive, both about the relationship and about themselves. For example, they may say, "My partner and I have such a strong relationship that even if (s)he finds someone else that (s)he thinks is better than me in some ways, (s)he will still want to continue the relationship with me." Or, "I am such a desirable person that even if my partner leaves me for someone else, I will be readily able to find an equally good new partner myself with whom to form an equally good relationship."

Partners who believe these optimistic worst-case outcomes to be true appear to have enough assurance in the relationship and themselves to risk non-exclusiveness. Conversely, people who lack confidence in their partner's commitment to them or who lack confidence in their own desirability are less likely to risk the potential loss of their current relationship that might result by opening it up to intimate involvement with others.

Non-possessive people tend to rank lower in terms of some personal attributes and values that are common in mainstream society. For the most part, the partners in non-monogamous relationships do not place much value on such concepts as duty, obedience, or sin and generally have lower than average needs for interpersonal power or controlling others.

Non-possessive adherents seem to be more easily able to adopt attitudes that are somewhat uncommon in the traditional culture. For example, they appear to rate highly in terms of cognitive flexibility. They seem to be able to shift their thinking from one perspective to another more readily than most traditional-relationship people who tend to have more attitudinal rigidity.

A prominent example of this flexibility in thinking is the ability of many non-possessive people to view love and sex as intertwined entities in some situations and yet separate activities in other situations. Thus, a non-monogamous individual seeing his/her beloved getting it on with someone else is able to keep calm and relax, (because) it's just sex.

Gender Differences: Benefits

"Vive la différence!"

—Traditional French toast

Men and women appear to have somewhat divergent risk/reward profiles when they become involved in non-possessive intimate relationships.

Both, of course, share many of the upsides in common. The obvious positives that both experience in similar ways may include the security of feeling bonded to someone who also wants to maintain a primary relationship and the caring, support, and nurturing of a loving partner.

Each gender must also cope with the downsides such as possible jealousy, the risk of loss, and all the what-ifs that come with non-possession. Nevertheless, in spite of these similarities, there seem to be benefit/cost factors that are specific to males and specific to females.

For most men, one of the most attractive features of a non-possessive intimate relationship is the "hall pass" benefit, meaning the implicit consent of his female partner that it would be alright, at least under certain limited circumstances, for him to have sex with other women.

For men, especially those who have been in an exclusive relationship for a long time, this license to roam may be very enticing. A husband may not even be very successful in attempting to exercise this freedom but just the fact that his wife is allowing him to act like a hunter and gatherer again can be enough reinforcement to prompt and maintain his willingness to engage in and continue with a non-possessive style of relationship.

If we accept the popular biological argument that the primary male imperative is to spread his seed as widely as possible, then the non-possessive intimate relationship option allows for at least some fulfillment of this innate drive. In addition, because the continued union of the couple is acknowledged and validated, it also permits the preservation of pair bonding, another strong biologic drive seen in many higher species.

Not only is the thrill of the chase a potent incentive for most men, but the culmination of the hunt is especially rewarding physiologically and psychologically. For most sexual encounters, "success" for the male is relatively easy to define as ejaculation while his penis is inside some orifice of a willing female. Men involved in non-possessive intimate relationships may have the opportunity to experience this success with as many women as possible.

Afterwards, men often experience satisfaction in relating the description of their "conquest" to other like-minded friends. So, for men, extramural sexual adventures can involve at least three stages of gratification: the seduction, the orgasm, and the high-five phases.

What's unique about non-possessive intimate relationships, especially as compared to traditional relationships, is that any or all of these satisfactions can be shared with the man's primary female partner! A supportive and experienced non-possessive wife may help recruit an external sex partner for her husband, may be physically present during his orgasm (e.g., in a threesome), and/or even be one of his drinking buddies enjoying the tale of his sexual exploits.

The clichéd husband/boyfriend lusting after other women while being reproached by the jealous wife/girlfriend may be transformed into a scenario in which, with the full awareness and support of the wife/girlfriend, the bonded male is given some agreed-upon freedom to pursue other females for limited encounters. In the most sophisticated of these arrangements, the wife/girlfriend may even assist her husband/boyfriend to identify, select, and seduce target females with the couple enjoying together the game-like aspects of the seduction. ("My wife is my wingman.")

In these advanced relationships, the husband/boyfriend is relatively free to enjoy other women sexually and not only maintain a loving bond with his long-time female companion but share his erotic adventures with her.

For women, the satisfactions from engaging in sexual and/or romantic encounters outside of a bonded relationship are similar to men's but distinctly different. Considering, for example, a wife who has been in a monogamous relationship for several years, the opportunity to re-explore intimate interactions with other men, with the approval of her husband, can be very enticing.

Three phases of potential gratification may also be seen for women in non-possessive relationships who are engaging in outside intimate encounters.

For women, a highly salient objective in these external activities is validating attractiveness. A monogamous wife, who has been out of the dating loop for some time, may wonder if she is still capable of attracting quality men. The chance to dress in provocative clothes and to practice, again, flirtatious behaviors may be quite exciting and rewarding, especially if she succeeds in obtaining desired male attention.

For women who engage in extra-relationship sexual/romantic activities, achieving orgasm is usually neither the defining event nor a criterion of success. Women, of course, experience sexual satisfactions in many ways other than solely coming to climax.

Considering the example of the previously monogamous wife now enjoying the erotic attentions of a new male lover, this experience can provide validation also that she can still feel heightened arousal that may have been missing or, at least, significantly diminished in her primary relationship. The fact that her primary mate has given his approval for her external liaison may allow her to relax and more fully enjoy her newly reawakened sensations.

Having an encounter with a new male lover, who is likely to be much more eager, responsive. and even more appreciative than her current primary partner, may serve to bolster flagging self-confidence in her womanliness. Bringing the male to his orgasm and receiving grateful compliments regarding her sexiness again may reinforce her self-image as being erotically skilled.

Sharing the story of last night's adventures involving the hot new guy with select girlfriends can be an additional source of satisfaction for the woman. With non-possessive relationships, an added plus is that the woman can share the details without fear of disclosure of the event to her primary male partner, because he likely already knows.

In fact, in non-possessive intimate relationships (strange as it may seem to the uninitiated), a husband can potentially be an active supporter and even participant in all phases of his wife's extramarital affairs.

A loving husband in such an arrangement might assist his wife in her quest for external erotic satisfactions in several ways. He may buy her revealing clothes, facilitate her contacts with potential new men, and offer reassurance of his love for her as she relates her outside adventures to him. Also, in threesomes (and moresomes), the husband may share pleasuring of his wife with other men concurrently.

These supportive actions that both of the partners in a non-possessive relationship provide for each other are, of course, in stark contrast to the hostilities commonly seen in possessive relationships when the threat of external sexual/romantic contact is perceived.

Overall, for a woman, the non-possessive lifestyle may offer the twin benefits of erotic adventure plus relationship security. She may find that she can be, at times, a free-range chicken and yet still come home to roost.

Gender Differences: Challenges

"Men never remember and women never forget."[9]

—Marianne Legato

For interactions between the partners in a non-possessive relationship to be sex-positive, the partners must overcome certain obstacles and manage some emotional, cognitive, and social risks. Some of these obstacles and hazards are similar for both men and women.

Doubts about the relationship, doubts about oneself, and jealousy are examples of challenges that both men and women may have to face in moving toward and sustaining non-possessiveness. Other risks, however, are more gender specific.

For men, breaking out of the double standard mold that many boys grow up with can be especially difficult. Men, who are typically socialized into roles that emphasize being guardians and protectors, often have trouble letting go of their ingrained need to defend what they may see as their most valuable "possession," their female, against the encroachment of competitor males.

It can be a source of amusement to those who are more experienced in the non-possessive lifestyle to observe the internal conflict in the possessive male brought about by the possibility of opening up his relationship. ("I *really* would love to be able to have approved sex with other women but to do so, I would have to let other men have sex with *my* woman. OMG, what should I do?")

A further risk, specific to men, is that of losing face with male peers for not enforcing a "no fly zone" policy around one's female partner. The competitiveness ethic among men often dictates that disrespect accrues to the man who does not or cannot protect his woman from interlopers.

A man, then, has to hedge against the dreaded "cuckold" label to maintain his own self-respect and that of his peers. The notion of willingly allowing your female partner to be "used" by other men is still so novel among traditional males as to generate incredulous reactions. ("You let your wife do *what*?!")

To these buddies, the defense of explaining to others that his female partner's liaisons are a result of permissiveness on his part, and not ignorance or inability, carries limited weight as a respect-bolstering strategy.

For a man with a wandering female partner (whether agreed to or not), the best ego defense and social rebuttal is to demonstrate, or at least claim, success of his own in hunting and gathering.

This quid pro quo (tit for tat?) argument may serve to protect a male's self-image adequately and may earn status points with other men. It can impress all but the most staunchly wedded to the traditional double standard, i.e., those who believe you should guard your cake and eat that of others too.

For a woman considering non-possessive alternatives for herself, the risks inherent in external explorations often are related to the potential loss of various forms of approval.

Chief among these hazards is the apprehension that if she does, in fact, engage in extra-relationship sexual/romantic activities, her primary partner may change his positive feelings toward her to a more negative perception. The woman in a newly-transitioned, non-possessive relationship heading out for her first overnight date with an outside lover may pose to her husband a variation of the familiar song lyric, "Will you still love me tomorrow?"

Women, who are often more intuitive and perceptive regarding emotional nuances, are usually quick to pick up any hint of ambivalence on the part of their primary male partner. A woman may guess that her partner, who is lustfully proposing outside encounters, may also be fearful of losing the exclusivity bond between herself and him. ("Is that you or is that the testosterone speaking?")

The apprehension that her primary partner may no longer consider her to be his one-and-only is often a major obstacle to a female partner considering the modification of their relationship to be less possessive.

The move toward non-possessiveness, which is most often proposed by the male partner, can even be viewed as a potential trap by the female partner. ("Could it be a test of my loyalty?") These and other similar negative possibilities seem to be especially salient concerns of women who are considering less possessive alternatives in their primary relationship.

The potential for loss of peer approval also weighs heavily on women considering a move to a more non-possessive form of their primary relationship. Almost all women are socialized into the belief that sex is permissible only within the bounds of a committed/exclusive relationship. To have sex outside of such a relationship, even with the explicit permission of the primary partner, may still be viewed as morally ambiguous at best by most women.

This form of disrespect may be an especially acute negative for women who rely heavily on support from their same-gender peers.

Women in this situation often attempt, successfully at times, to portray this criticism from girlfriends and other females they are close to as arising out of their jealousy due these women still being "trapped" in possessive relationships. Alternatively, some women are successful in achieving support by forming social networks with others in the same lifestyle.

Nevertheless, the woman choosing to become involved in non-possessive intimate activities risks having her reputation called into question and being called uncomplimentary names, by both genders, as a result of her atypical relationship orientation.

Just as other unconventional and/or marginalized people have embraced and positivized formerly negative epithets (for example, the recent trends toward self-definition as "queer" by some gays and "nigger" by some blacks), so have some in the non-possessive subculture embraced the pejorative terms used against them and turned the nasty words into self-affirmation by "reclaiming" them.

These sex-positive pioneers have also emphasized the moral virtues of non-possessive relationships, emphasizing such values as truthfulness, trust, and harm avoidance. The best presentation of this position is *The Ethical Slut*.[10] The authors are two women who are role models for others searching for ways to live and love unconventionally, with integrity.

CHAPTER FIVE

Practical Matters

Anyone involved intimately with anyone else has many relationship management practicalities to contend with. Non-possessive people often manage some of these challenges differently than those who are monogamous.

In addition to the universal issues, people who are actively involved in non-possessive intimate relationships find that they must also deal with a whole host of matters with which those in more traditional unions never have to cope.

Restrictions

> *"#10. Thou shalt not covet thy neighbor's wife.*
> *(Nor thy neighbor's maidservant!)"*[1]

—Moses

All relationships have proscriptive and prohibitive aspects to their defining agreement. Although what you *should* do in an intimate relationship is clearly regarded as of some significance, the really important clauses are usually in the "Thou shalt not" section of the contract. (See the Ten Commandments.)

Relationships may be seen as varying along a continuum representing the number and type of limitations agreed to by the partners regarding intimate contact with others. Restrictions can range from total, as in an exclusive, conservative relationship, to none, as in a no-limits type of arrangement.

Although there is a common misperception that non-possessive people are unrestrained total hedonists, in fact, virtually all operate within the context of agreed-upon restrictions. In terms of the above continuum, most non-exclusive couples are somewhere in the middle, adopting some limitations but not too many.

Transitioning to a less possessive form of a relationship essentially requires the partners of a couple to reconfront issues, such as safe sex and unwanted pregnancy, that they may not have had to consider since they were single. Most couples seem to make this transition successfully and are able to keep the inherent risks low enough so as not to offset the perceived rewards.

Some couples choose to leave their agreement regarding extramural activities unstated, preferring a sort of "Don't Ask, Don't Tell" policy. To avoid miscommunications, however, most non-possessive couples prefer that their understanding is more clearly specified, at least in terms of basic parameters.

Most limitations are agreed upon to protect the safety of the externally engaging partner and the sensitivities of the other partner. Agreements regarding involvements with outsiders generally include some of the following issues:

- Choice of lovers, as in these are OK, but those are not.
- Frequency of external encounters—e.g., whenever, one per month, birthday present.
- Where—e.g., never in conjugal bed, only when out of town.
- Pre-approval or pre-notification needed?
- Post-event reporting required, with or without detail?
- Activity taboos, for example, condom essential, no anal, and so on.

By making restrictions explicit, non-possessive couples essentially balance the freedom to indulge outside the relationship with a list of responsibilities. This process allows for some sense of security for the partners in that each may feel more relaxed and able to enjoy their external encounters, knowing that they should not be criticized by their primary partner as long as they have followed the rules of engagement.

As an example of one type of restriction, most non-possessive couples agree on some activity limitations to protect against sexually transmitted infections. STIs are not generally an issue in a completely monogamous relationship. (This is one of the reasons most cited by conservative couples for preferring exclusivity.) Once outsiders become involved, however, contracting STIs becomes a possibility and managing this risk is one of the most common topics for restriction-agreement discussion.

Mandatory use of condoms is the most frequent requirement. Although most participants in consensual extra-partner activities practice safe sex in this way, some prefer the sensations of barrier-free stimulation (often called "bareback riding").

Care in selecting external parties to engage with is another frequent requirement. Similar to "best practices" in the porn industry, some couples active in outside encounters undergo regular STI screenings to confirm and document their disease-free status and some request similar clearance reports from potential external candidates.

Across the many varieties of non-possessive intimate relationships, there does not seem to be any undue concern with the potential for adverse biological effects. Although relevant studies are notoriously lacking in credibility, there does not appear to be any compelling evidence that STI prevalence rates or unwanted pregnancies, for example, are any higher in those who are non-possessive than in those with more traditional, exclusive relationships.[2] (This result is understandable considering the high frequency of assignations with secret lovers among traditional couples.)

In spite of the fact that many non-possessives may routinely have a lot of sex with a lot of different people, getting an STI is generally an outcome with a low probability and a low level of concern. To a large extent, this somewhat counterintuitive correlation may be explained by social factors.

Among non-possessives, much extra-relationship intimate activity takes place within the context of small social networks, such as swing clubs or polyamory associations. Values emphasizing non-harmful behavior are commonly held by members who communicate with each other regularly. Anyone acting irresponsibly may be quickly identified and ostracized.

Selectivity

"With great power must come great responsibility."[3]
—Spiderman (with apologies to Voltaire)

For those who are considering the exploration of less possessive relationships, a common concern (especially for women) and a common fantasy (especially for men) is that sexual encounters may become indiscriminate. Those unfamiliar with the social dynamics of recreational sex communities, for example, may experience the apprehension and/or hope that they may have to, or be able to, engage in sexual activity with anyone at any time.

With some experience, however, newcomers learn that being non-possessive about sex doesn't mean acting without choices of when, where, how, and especially, with whom. In fact, in the world of non-possessive intimate encounters, selectivity issues may become magnified.

More specifically, the transition from a traditional to a less possessive form of a relationship may often entail some significant shifts for a typical couple in the way the partners relate to selection decisions regarding outsiders.

When one is involved in monogamous relationships, one has built-in boundaries to one's sexual activities. ("I can't have sex with you because I'm married, have a boy/girlfriend, etc.") Once one opens the boundaries of these possessive relationships, however, these protestations can no longer serve as automatic exemptions from engaging in new sexual encounters.

When people choose to be non-possessive of and non-possessed by their primary partners, they experience not only the freedom to attempt to engage with whomever they may want to but also the necessity of making choices now that they would not have had to make previously. For some, especially those who may have felt protected by the restrictions inherent in possessive relationships, this new freedom/obligation can be perceived as challenging or even threatening.

Those who value sexual freedom do not generally engage in erotic activities indiscriminately. Although there may be some situational exceptions, typically, a lot of choices are made as to whom to participate with and under what circumstances. Even the most adventuresome still select some people and some situations and reject others.

The factors influencing selection among non-possessive individuals are much the same as those that are salient for people who are more exclusive in their intimate relationships. Equally prominent for both are the characteristics of potential candidates such as perceived attractiveness, skillfulness, willingness, and so on.

Compared to the factors operating in the more traditional mate selection process, however, there is little or no concern about long-term issues. When non-possessive individuals are sizing each other up to determine potential compatibility for an erotic encounter, there is relatively minimal consideration of questions such as, "Will he be a good provider?" or "Can she cook?"

The freedom to select sexual partners without having to factor in long-term potential, as would be the case in the traditional mate-hunting process, is often cited as a very positive feature of the non-possessive lifestyle, especially by women.

Traditional relationships often require some trade-offs for women who may have to give up some erotic features in a potential mate in order to obtain one with more stable attributes. Within the non-possessive communities, both genders, but especially women, are free to seek that elusive "great sex" experience as an end in and of itself.

A somewhat novel variant of the selection process occurs in the "Lifestyle" community, in which couples choose other couples for exchanging partners. In traditional dating/mating selection rituals, individuals make individual positive/negative decisions. In the swing-couples scene, for example, the dynamics of selection get more complex and become a 2×2 decision matrix, with all cells needing to come up positive for lift-off to occur.

Although there can be exceptions, typically all four members of the two couples need to agree on the potential swap before it can happen. At times, one member may veto the proposed liaison, often because that member's prospective sex-partner is perceived as not being sufficiently attractive, skillful, etc. Again, as in the singles situation, women tend to be the primary go/no-go decision makers in these transactions.

The veto potential can lead to conflict within at least one couple, as well as opportunities for negotiation, compromises, trade-offs, and the like. The sports analogy of "taking one for the team" is frequently invoked in this context and, as in baseball, a player's trade can be made with the promise of future considerations.

Communication

"What we've got here is a failure to communicate."[4]

—*Cool Hand Luke*

Good communication is probably the single most important process a couple can engage in (even more important than good sex!). To be "good," communication should be:

- Honest—speaking the truth and avoiding deception.
- Assertive—identifying thoughts and feelings and conveying them accurately.
- Timely—appropriate to the time, place, and context.

These features may well be present in any type of relationship but non-possessive couples often report enhanced awareness and usage of these positive communication attributes as compared to more possessive couples.

This may be because the process of crafting and implementing a non-exclusive agreement usually entails a rather intense focus on keeping each other closely informed about each other's thoughts, feelings, past actions, and future intentions. Many non-possessive couples find that this exercise spills over into other areas of their relationship and they become better communicators generally.

Also, the removal of the strict taboo regarding outside erotic and/or romantic contacts eliminates a major class of opportunities for deception, unassertiveness, and other covert processes that interfere with good communication.

The partners in many monogamous couples may talk openly with each other in most areas except for sex and, especially, for thoughts, feelings, and actions regarding erotic contact with outsiders. Most non-possessive couples are able to talk honestly regarding the sex-with-others topic and, as a result, their clear communication agenda is less restricted.

In any relationship, good communication is facilitated when there is a structured opportunity for check-in with each other regarding thoughts, feelings, and actions. Many non-possessive couples do a routine "debriefing" session following any external encounters.

These can serve as training sessions in which the partners practice their skills in communicating honestly and assertively. They may find that these enhanced skills generalize to other areas in which there is potential for emotional reactivity.

Some couples parlay this approach into a kind of a relationship co-therapy in which they engage in regular state-of-the-relationship discussions focusing on all aspects of their interaction.

In a model that I recommend, couples set aside a fixed time each week to have a "Gardening Session" in which they review issues, both positive and negative, that have arisen since the last time. The metaphor here is to water the flowers that grow in the garden of their relationship but also to pull out any weeds that may have infiltrated.

Communication between the primary partners is important also when decisions need to be made regarding selection of outside hook-ups. At a swing party, for example, one couple may meet another couple and mutual flirting may ensue. At some point, choices may need to be made as to whether to proceed with more intimate connections or not.

Essentially, each member of each couple needs to communicate with their primary partner regarding their preference for proceeding. In the most cautious scenario, each couple may huddle separately and debate the pros and cons of proceeding with the other couple. This process can often be socially awkward, however, (especially if one couple's decision is negative) when rejoining the other couple to convey the verdict.

As a result, the partners of experienced couples often develop short-hand systems of discreet communication with each other so that each may express their level of interest in a possible liaison with their opposite member in the new couple, while still chatting with them.

Frequently, these communications are coded or masked in some way so as to avoid potential embarrassment if any one of the four parties involved does not want to proceed. ("Honey, is it hot in this room or is it just me?"—"Oh, I don't know sweetie, I'm feeling a little chilly, actually.")

Secrecy

"I want the truth!"

—Lt. Kaffee

"You can't handle the truth!!"[5]

—Col. Jessup

The partners of a couple involved in a non-possessive intimate relationship must confront the issue of revealing their status to traditionally-minded others, who may be very disapproving of their "aberrant" arrangement. Such couples struggle with the dilemma of how much to disclose and to whom.

They have to cope with matters similar to those experienced by gays coming out about their sexual orientation. ("Should we tell our family members, our children, our friends, our co-workers, and others, and if so, which ones and how much should we tell them?")

Many couples opt for total secrecy about the unorthodox form of their relationship while others are completely open about being open. Each approach has its associated benefits and perils.

With the non-disclosure option, it may seem like there would be no potentially embarrassing questions to answer but the couple may end up lying to everyone they know about their relationship and about their outside lover(s). ("Mommy, why does Uncle George stay overnight with us?")

The inevitable deceptions are similar to those experienced by the partners of couples in which one or both are having covert affairs. In the consensual non-monogamous situation, however, both partners are in on the same ruse, which is only maintained for outsiders.

Well-meaning friends can, at times, pick up clues regarding a partner's seemingly suspicious behavior. Assuming a traditional possessive relationship, the friends may conclude that the one partner is cheating and attempt to warn or console the other.

This scenario can lead to potentially amusing situations in which the partner being told must figure out how to respond to the news of the other partner's alleged "infidelity" without spilling the beans that (s)he knew and approved of it all along. (There are enough romantic comedy possibilities in this setup that there must be a Hollywood screenplay in there somewhere.)

Opportunities for levity aside, the total secrecy strategy can create significant stress for the couple who need to constantly guard their activities from outsiders. When both partners are very active externally, this stress can be more complex, if not more intense, than that experienced when one partner is having a covert liaison.

On the other hand, the very fact of having shared secrets kept from the rest of the world can be a bonding element, strengthening the couple's relationship. ("If only they knew, wouldn't they think we were scandalous?")

Similarly, having a covert identity and being part of an underground counter-culture can serve as a powerful shared connection for the partners in a non-possessive relationship. Just like superheroes, they may see themselves as putting on their (club clothes) costumes and going off into the night to fight the evils of sexual repression.

The shared secrecy option not only protects the couple from the disapproval of others but can also be interpreted by the couple as serving to protect outsiders from having to encounter attitudes and behavior that others may find upsetting or even threatening (for example, to "family values," etc.). In this way, the "you can't handle the truth" position may be seen by the couple as a noble act that may further serve to reinforce their sense of superiority vis-à-vis the "vanilla" world.

Disclosure to Others

"The Book of Life *begins with a man and a woman in a garden.*
It ends with Revelations."[6]

—Oscar Wilde

For those couples who choose to be more upfront about their non-possessive intimate relationship, the good news is that, in doing so, they can avoid the stress of having to be deceptive to others they are close to. The bad news is that they may trade that type of stress for the stress caused by the potential disapproval of those they care about.

Again, similar to any person who engages in any type of atypical sexual/romantic activities, coming out about one's "deviancy" places one at risk for negative reactions from others with intolerant perspectives. ("How could you voluntarily let your husband run around with other women?")

Reactions from others let in on the couple's non-possessive intimate relationship style, may range broadly from mild curiosity to extreme hostility. The latter response is sometimes encountered from religious conservatives who see the couple's openness as a direct threat to the sanctity of marriage, the purity of womanhood, and so on. ("The devil probably made them do it.")

Couples who have disclosed that they have a non-possessive intimate relationship have been shunned by former friends, berated by otherwise caring family members, and even fired from their jobs.[7] At some point, the reactions of outsiders who are negative tend to focus on accusing the couple of being immoral, sinful, and so on, for violating such obvious (to the accusers) societal mores. ("But what about the effects on the children?")

To withstand such social disapprobation and to cope successfully with the negative reactions that disclosure brings, the couple with a non-possessive intimate relationship must have good defense mechanisms in place to counter feelings of guilt, shame, and more.

In their defense, articulate couples in non-possessive intimate relationships may point out that their arrangement is a sex-positive win-win-win solution for all concerned and is based on love, honesty, and good communication. They may add that it is ironic that in our society where the dishonesty and betrayal implicit in covert affairs is often greeted with a wink and a nod by sophisticated friends, something as truthful and supportive as consensual non-monogamy is reacted to so negatively.

Couples in non-possessive intimate relationships who have some familiarity with psychodynamic concepts may suggest to their detractors that extreme negative reactions to their non-traditional orientation may, like similar reactions to homosexuality, be rooted in fears of becoming like that or as a defense against unacceptable wishes to be more sexually adventuresome with others.

On a more potentially amusing level, the partners of a couple disclosing themselves to be non-possessive may find themselves having to deal with unexpected or unwanted invitations from others who may assume they are freely available and willing. ("Say, if your husband doesn't mind then, why don't we get together for a drink after work?")

Some couples have a need to push the envelope of disclosure and make a political statement about their non-possessiveness, proselytizing to all who will listen and extolling the joys of their unconventional arrangement. These couples see themselves as being in the vanguard of a new open-relationship "movement" and want to use their own non-possessive style as a demonstration model for others to follow. Like all crusaders, they often bear the brunt of attacks by moral absolutists and may experience negative personal consequences for their high-profile love-style.

Most non-monogamous couples choose a disclosure comfort zone somewhere along the continuum between the polar alternatives of total secrecy and total openness. The typical non-possessive couple may share their secret with a few trusted friends and/or family members but maintain the confidentiality of their arrangement in dealing with everyone else.

Determining who to disclose to can be daunting (but also amusing at times) as the couple may face misunderstandings on the part of those friends to whom they are considering disclosing. ("If we tell them what we do, they may think we are trying to get into bed with them too.")

The first disclosure to a specific person is often viewed as a trust exercise and the outcome can add insights to the couple's relationship with the person(s) to whom they are revealing their status.

Often, the couple assessing whether or not to disclose will prompt a discussion of non-possessiveness in the media as a way of evaluating reactions. ("Say, we've got this funny old movie called *Bob & Carol & Ted & Alice*.[8] Why don't we all get together to watch it and have some laughs?")

Desirability/Performance Issues

"Looking good is better than feeling good."[9]
                                        —Billy Crystal (as Fernando Lamas)

Among possessive couples, a common motivation for restricting sex to one's partner only is the concern regarding sexual performance and/or desirability. A person who perceives him/herself as not very skillful sexually or desirable may want to prohibit his/her partner from comparison shopping.

Performance anxiety, especially among men, and worries regarding sexual desirability, especially among women, may contribute significantly to a couple's decision to maintain a monogamous relationship.

Among non-possessive couples, however, concerns regarding sexual adequacy and desirability seem to be much less prevalent. People involved in non-monogamous relationships generally have more sexual activity, both in terms of frequency and variety. As a result, they appear to be more confident regarding their capability and attractiveness as a sex partner.

There is most likely a positive-reinforcement cycle at work here with those people having a more secure sexual self-image seeking a less possessive style and then the frequency and variety experienced with that choice further enhancing their self-confidence. Possessive couples, conversely, may spiral downward in a more negatively-reinforcing cycle with less frequency and variety creating even more doubts and concerns regarding sexual performance and desirability.

The various "tribes" of those committed to non-possessiveness, such as swingers, polyamorists, recreational sex adherents, and so on, may reflect a kind of Darwinian process, at least in terms of the evolution of behaviors in the individual organism.

In a sort of a survival of the sexually fittest way, these groups tend to be made up of people who have some of the highest levels of sexual performance and self-confidence regarding their attractiveness. As such, they often regard themselves as the alpha males and females sexually, as compared to the general population.

Couples and individuals with high levels of sex drive, performance skills, and self-confidence gravitate to non-possessive lifestyles. Others, with lower levels of these factors, generally do not explore these options.

Some less capable and/or less attractive individuals or couples may attempt to participate in various non-possessive venues and activities. Their limitations may result in failure experiences, however, resulting in a self-generated weeding-out effect.

Alternatively, some people who describe themselves as having been clueless, nerdy, and so on, report very significant growth initially, over time, in self-confidence and performance skills with repeated practice and experience in sexual sharing. A facilitating factor here is the inclusiveness and acceptance of many of the non-possessive sub-cultures, which tend to be very welcoming to newcomers, regardless of their initial abilities or attractiveness, as long as the newbies have a sex-positive attitude.

In any event, the net result of this natural selection process is the creation of a large pool of individuals and couples who are highly motivated to engage intimately with others and who are highly capable of doing so skillfully. The discovery of such an attractive sub-population by those who have strong similar needs and capabilities can come as a revelation.

For a man, there is an obvious delight in discovering situations in which there are significant numbers of attractive women who may be willing and even eager to have non-commercial sex with him. The fact that the vast majority of these women are simply seeking a sexual peak experience, rather than mate hunting, just adds to the allure of these recreational sex situations.

For a woman, the natural selection process usually results in a kind of quality-control effect. In the "vanilla" world, women who are sizing up a potential sex partner must cope with questions such as, "Is he going to be sensitive to my needs, a skillful lover, not abusive, and so on?" In many of the well-organized non-possessive venues, most of the men with negative attributes have already been screened out.

Consequently, a woman can often choose from a pool of desirable candidates knowing that her chances of having a disappointing experience are greatly reduced. More positively, having such a competent and attentive group of men available to choose from greatly enhances her chances of achieving the elusive "great sex" experience.

For those with high sex drives of both genders, when first coming into contact with these various non-possessive lifestyles, the reaction is often, "OMG, what a bonanza! Where have these people been all my life?"

People who enjoy good food and fine wine are often delighted to discover others who share these interests. Similarly, many people in the various non-possessive affiliations may be considered connoisseurs of high-quality sex and actively seek to connect with others to share their passion for peak experiences in this area. (Perhaps similar to wine-tastings, some recreational sex venues stage erotic "speed dating" events in which participants may sample each other briefly.)

Unequal Participation

"What's sauce for the goose is (not necessarily) sauce for the gander."[10]
—Old English proverb

For some couples, the motivation to engage in external sex may be much greater in one partner than the other. Traditional-relationship couples often handle these situations badly, with the usual triple-D outcomes of deception, dishonesty, and dissolution. Non-possessive couples have been innovative in exploring more positive models of managing unequal needs.

In one of these adaptations, one partner (for example, the wife) may not be especially interested in participating herself but she will accompany her husband to recreational sex venues (which may require a couple for admission). In this way, she enables his participation with other women while remaining a spectator herself.

In this variation, by being non-possessive, the wife may express loving kindness to her husband in allowing and encouraging him to participate in an activity she knows he will greatly enjoy. Not being entirely altruistic, the wife may obtain some gratitude from her husband in return and/or may trade-off for some escorted activity of her own. ("So after we're finished at the club, let's go sign up for that jewelry-making cruise!")

Some unequal-participation couples have evolved an arrangement whereby the husband, for example, engaging in outside erotic encounters (with the approval of the wife) brings her a gift after each encounter as "penance." The "aggrieved" wife in these situations could amass quite a substantial collection of presents to display to her girlfriend confidants. ("This is the necklace he got me after his weekend with Dolly and this is the bracelet I got after Carmen, and. . . .")

In another unequal participation variation, a man (perhaps older) may not be capable of much engagement sexually with other women but may allow and encourage his (perhaps much younger) girlfriend to do so. In this way, the man can give his female partner the gift of sex with others to help satisfy her greater need for erotic activity.

Although it may seem counterintuitive to most traditionalists, such men often report considerable personal satisfaction regarding several aspects of such an arrangement. Among these may be the pleasurable anticipation in buying the female partner sexy clothes, helping her get dressed for her "date," excitement in hearing later of her adventures, and satisfying sex with her afterwards as a result of the heightened arousal of both partners.

For those unfamiliar with this dynamic among certain couples, this type of candaulism may seem to be so odd as to be quite rare. As evidence of its popularity, however, it seems to have spawned a whole subgenre of erotic literature. (See any issue of *Penthouse Letters*,[11] especially the section titled, "Take Her, She's Mine.")

All of these creative alternatives to satisfying unequal needs represent a kind of outsourcing of the sexual aspects of the relationship. By using this approach, the non-possessive couple attempts to protect the bonding between the primary partners with all of its positive nonsexual aspects.

By getting the more needful partner's needs met in a mutually approved way, the couple hopes to reduce the likelihood that that partner will be motivated to look for unapproved sources of fulfillment.

Unequal erotic participation is often seen also in stable threesomes and polyamorous groupings. These multi-partner arrangements frequently arise from situations in which one partner of an existing couple is much less interested in sex than the other, for example. In this setting, a third participant may be recruited to fill this need of the deprived partner.

Long-lasting, living-together triads can thus be formed in which there may be a sort of division of labor, with one same-gender partner specializing in the non-sexual aspects of intimacy in the three-way relationship and the other taking care of the sexual aspects. (Some scheduling of household chores may be necessary.)

Risk Management

"Risk comes from not knowing what you're doing."[12]

—Warren Buffett

Couples who choose to restructure their relationship to be non-possessive face certain hazards, both to the partnership and to each partner individually. If the new arrangement turns out badly, these risks may include loss of support from one's partner or friends, loss of self-esteem, or even loss of the relationship itself. Couples who are successful in developing and maintaining a non-possessive relationship find ways to hedge against these hazards.

Successful non-possessive couples must also find ways to obtain sufficient positive reinforcement for the partners to make the taking on the risks tolerable. So each couple, in effect, engages in a kind of cost/benefit analysis as to the possibility of opening up their relationship to be less possessive. This analysis tends to be ongoing as the couple explores their boundaries involving intimate relationships with others.

If insecurity in the relationship is prominent, for example, the partners may perceive the threat of loss of the partnership as being too great to risk exploring less possessive alternatives. Conversely, if the partners feel that their relationship is strong, stable, and resilient, they may be more willing to consider a less traditional arrangement.

Similarly, if one or both of the partners has doubts about their own self-worth, opening up the relationship may pose unacceptable risks, in that one may be seen by one's partner as less desirable than some potential new lover. Again, if the threat level is judged to be too high, a move toward non-possessiveness will not be a viable option.

The fear of abandonment is probably the single biggest reason that the partners in traditional relationships mandate sexual fidelity. Many people in a possessive arrangement feel that if their partner ever had the opportunity to sample anyone else sexually, the partner might run off with the outsider, leaving themselves to cope with loneliness, embarrassment, anger, etc.

Non-possessive individuals appear to be more confident regarding their sexual abilities and seem to be less apprehensive about having their partner conduct a comparison test.

Even in the worst-case scenario, if one partner does leave, the remaining partner in a non-possessive arrangement generally feels attractive and confident enough to be able to acquire and develop a new relationship. In fact, the abandoned partner may have already a few possibilities among their existing external lovers.

The partners of those couples who engage in non-possessive relationships are generally not risk averse. They are likely to be more adventuresome and stimulus seeking than the average person. As a result, they tend to have a history of learning and developing strategies of how best to mitigate loss potential.

Many couples exploring the transition to a less possessive structure to their relationship develop some type of understandings to hedge against the emotional perils of external intimacies. Similar to pre-nuptial agreements, these (pre-nookie?) agreements often attempt to assess and manage the ongoing feelings of each partner toward outsiders with whom the partners may become intimately involved.

Although agreements can be made in an attempt to minimize emotional, long-term ties to others, these pacts offer only limited liability against loss. Passion can trump reason, obviously, and even a well-intentioned person can find themselves sliding down the slippery slope of increased commitment to an external person, especially one with whom they are having (great) sex.

In addition to an upfront agreement to avoid external emotional entanglements, the partners of most successful non-possessive couples may develop procedures to monitor each other's feelings, sometimes quite carefully.

Often, the partners engage in regular communication sessions in which each one reports their thoughts, feelings, and actions involving intimate activities with outsiders. At the very least, this type of communication allows each partner to keep informed regarding the status of their primary partner and to use that information to make rational decisions regarding future courses of action.

If there is, indeed, full disclosure along the way, the process of one partner developing an attachment to someone else, if it does occur, tends to be gradual and usually avoids the unpleasant sudden surprise typical in a traditional relationship when a covert affair is discovered.

By being assertive and truthful, the partners at least show care and respect for each other in the event that there is eventual separation between them. Often, because feelings of betrayal are eliminated or at least reduced, many non-possessive couples find they can continue to have an emotionally and/or physically intimate relationship even after one or both have moved on to other primary partners.

Moving toward a more polyamorous type of relationship may be seen as another type of risk management strategy. Many poly individuals and couples see the cause and effect relationship between sex and love not as a threat but as a natural and positive aspect, not only of this lifestyle, but of human nature in general. Instead of attempting to limit any one partner's involvement with anyone else, a polyamorous person may concentrate their efforts on finding additional love interests for themselves.

Truly polyamorous people are able to develop and maintain genuine love relationships with more than one partner at a time. This approach may represent a kind of diversification strategy in which the hedge against the loss of any one lover is to have others already present in your intimacy investment portfolio.

Commonality Characteristics

"Love does not consist in gazing at each other,
But in looking outward together in the same direction."[13]

—Antoine de Saint-Exupéry

Although there is an almost infinite variety of ways in which people can structure sexual/romantic relationships, those in which each partner does not attempt to enforce ownership of the other's intimate activities appear to have several traits in common. Certain values and communication patterns appear to be widely shared across almost all variants of non-possessive intimate relationships.

Just as with traditional relationships, less possessive couples have many shared aspects of their union which operate to create a kind of pair bonding. Emotional intimacy, shared values, and a common history serve as adhesives holding the couple together in virtually all non-possessive intimate relationships. Many of these features of their relationship they share only with each other.

What's unique about these non-possessive couples, however, is their willingness and ability to consider sexual and/or romantic activities as being not necessarily exclusive to the partner-only relationship.

All relationships involve some sort of agreement that defines how the partners should and should not relate to one another and to outsiders.

Unlike contract-equivalent pre-nuptials, however, most agreements in traditional intimate relationships are implied, implicit, and may often be unspoken. Typically, they are understood as an integral part of the couple culture and are often referenced by code words, such as "commitment."

Much in the same way as discount airlines have explored unbundling their fare structure in allowing passengers to choose and pay for only those services they want, adventuresome non-possessive couples have deconstructed the traditional relationship agreement, keeping the parts they want for themselves and making the others optional.

So, the agreements forged by non-possessive couples tend to be more explicitly specified and may often be the result of some analysis of the strengths and needs of the relationship and the partners. In this way, these couples are often more thoughtful and analytic about their partnership than traditional couples.

Central to the non-possessive relationship is the concept of selection by each partner as to how to implement their non-exclusivity. The partners typically agree that for those aspects of their relationship that are deemed to be allowable for external engagements (usually erotic/romantic activities), each partner shall choose how, where, when, and with whom to engage.

Although each partner may exercise some veto power vis-à-vis the parameters of some activities or the characteristics of some potential playmates (male or female), in general, each partner's right to choose what they believe would be most satisfying to them is recognized and supported.

Consensual decision-making is another key element in almost all non-possessive intimate relationships. Consensus means that both partners are aware of the outside activities and agree to the arrangements.

If extra-relationship, erotic/romantic activities occur and these are not agreed upon, then there is no consensus. These activities would likely fall into the category of "double standard," if the other partner is aware of the activities or "cheating," if the other partner is not aware.

Open and honest communication between the partners is a very important value to almost all couples involved in non-possessive intimate relationships. Unless otherwise agreed to, each partner routinely informs the other regarding any external liaisons. Some of these couples also schedule regular discussion sessions to explore thoughts and feelings regarding recent or planned activities.

Full disclosure may or may not be extended to external lovers, however. Some partners are very conscientious about informing potential new boy/girlfriends about the non-possessive nature of their primary relationship. Others choose to withhold this information, at least in the case of more transitory encounters.

The revealing of one's sexual and emotional connections is an important value in the polyamory community, however, where it is felt that this knowledge is necessary for all to make fully informed choices.

When they dabble in the dating scene, however, the partners of some non-possessive couples may choose to present themselves more covertly. They often feel a need to protect others from TMI (too much information) or from exposing others to situations that may be too novel/complex for the others to feel comfortable. So, a wife in one of these couples may slip off her wedding ring when she goes out for a night of trolling at the singles bar.

Honesty and full disclosure between the partners can, at times, serve purposes other than those that may be entirely altruistic or intended solely to inform one's partner. Sophisticated non-possessive couples may tweak these communications with the intent of creating arousal or even to prompt a bit of creative jealousy in their partner.

Consider, for example, the husband who tells his wife, "Sweetie, I hope you don't mind but last night, I had sex with your best friend and she was great!"

Or better perhaps, the wife who replies, "Well that's wonderful, dear, and by the way, last week, when you couldn't make it to your poker game, I went in your place and had a great time there playing with all of your buddies."

Prerequisites for Non-Possessiveness

"What is it men in women do require?
The lineaments of gratified desire.
What is it women do in men require?
The lineaments of gratified desire."[14]

—William Blake

Some couples are able to transition seamlessly from a traditional to a less exclusive form of their relationship. Others struggle with the transition, encounter significant negative experiences, and give up. Certain pre-existing qualities, both of the individuals involved and of the relationship itself, appear to predict success in developing a non-possessive intimate partnership and making it work pragmatically and emotionally for the couple.

When a couple first starts to explore less possessive options in their relationship, they often begin with an attempt at an honest evaluation of its current status. This usually proceeds along the lines of, "I love you, but. . . ." At this time, issues of fading passion, lack of opportunity for erotic stimulation, boredom due to routine encounters, and so forth may be aired.

For this and subsequent discussions to be productive, one essential prerequisite is for the partners to be assertive with each other. Assertiveness generally has at least two components:

1.   The ability to identify your true feelings, and
2.   The willingness to communicate these feelings to someone else.

Effective assertiveness requires emotional honesty. To be truly assertive, a person needs to be able to perceive clearly how they feel. For some people, this emotional honesty does not come easily, especially when one is dealing with potentially charged issues such as sex and love.

Effective assertiveness also requires the ability to verbalize one's feelings in a way that is straightforward and descriptive rather than interpretive or blaming. Assertive statements often take the form, "When you do A, I feel B."

Honest and direct communication is not necessarily part of the skill set of a lot of couples. Many people grow up being reinforced for learning devious communication patterns intended to gain advantage by deceiving others.

For those couples who do not have experience or facility with assertive communication, the good news is that self-help books, training workshops, and other resources are widely available. In general, those couples whose communication patterns do not include the ability to be truly assertive have difficulty creating a non-possessive intimate relationship that will work well for them.

Another prerequisite that appears to be highly important in determining the chances of success in a couple moving toward less possessiveness is the level of trust present in the relationship. The partners of a couple who have a high level of trust in each other are more able to discuss and explore non-possessive alternatives and to make these options work for them.

"Trust" may be defined as the degree of confidence we have in predicting the behavior of another person in a given situation. Trust is primarily a function of past experience. If previously you have always kept your promises, I can predict, with a high degree of probability, that you will keep them in the future.

It may be possible to rate the level of trust in any relationship along a scale from never to always. If, in the past, there have been breaches of trust, such as secret affairs, the couple may have a low trust index score and one or both of the partners may be very sensitive to possible violations of whatever agreements are made.

Conversely, couples with a high degree of confidence in predicting each other's agreement-compliance behavior are more likely to succeed in creating and maintaining a non-possessive version of their relationship. This is true even in those situations in which compliance is not 100 percent but the exceptions are, at least, well understood. ("My husband is very faithful to me unless he sees a woman with huge breasts; then he totally loses it.")

Cognitive and emotional flexibility also appear to be important personal characteristics which predict success in couples exploring alternate options of relating intimately with others. In particular, it is likely essential for the partners to be able to separate sex from love and to learn to be able, at times, to think and feel some differentiation of these two aspects of their relationship.

For most people, especially women, these two aspects are inextricably bound together, a belief that is usually the result of extensive social programming. Although many single people, especially men, can quite readily engage in sex without having love as part of the package, this becomes more difficult, or at least more complex, when one is part of a bonded relationship.

The novel concept that in a marriage, for example, sex could be partitioned from love can be a bit of a revelation for many couples. The idea that you could have consensually-approved sex with other people, with the full knowledge and even support of your spouse or significant other and still love and make love with your primary partner seems, at first, to be a radical notion to most people. And yet, many couples are doing just this and their relationships are flourishing as a result.

Couples who are successful in establishing a non-possessive partnership generally have succeeded in redefining sex as a stand-alone activity that can be engaged in for its own sake and not only or necessarily as a demonstration of love.

The cognitive flexibility inherent in this shift may require the couple to think outside the usual bounds of societal, religious, and even moral values. These couples often develop a unique set of personal ethics that emphasize factors other than sex as the defining criteria of their relationship.

Clinically, the partners of successful non-possessive couples seem to have a low incidence of anxiety, adjustment, or personality disorders. It is rare to see in these individuals, for example, instances of histrionic behaviors (such as the dreaded "drama queen" syndrome).

For the most part, non-possessive individuals tend to be calm, easygoing, and not overly excitable. They appear to be able to treat playfully, matters such as physical intimacies, which others regard much more seriously. As a result, they are able to relax, because a sense of playfulness pervades much of the interactive style among non-possessive people. Sex in the "vanilla" world is usually conducted without much, if any, humor and can even be somewhat grim business, at times.

By contrast, non-possessive people frequently joke and laugh about sexual intimacies, sometimes even when they are engaged in them! Consider, for example, the following conversation between a man and a woman who have just met at a club and are about to make "the beast with two backs":

She: It's time for you to put on a condom.
He: OK, but you have to tell me a condom joke while I'm doing it.
She: I know you're a stockbroker, so I'll pass on to you a market tip that I got yesterday. A friend of mine who lives in Tokyo and follows the Nikkei (the Japanese stock market index) called to tell me that there was a big story about to break. He said that a huge Japanese novelty manufacturer (the one that uses those cute little felines as their logo) is just about ready to announce the marketing of a new product line that is going to be a blockbuster. According to his inside sources, they have been secretly working on the development of "adult" supplies, including sex

toys. What a surprise! And here's where it ties in to your request. Their first product release is going to be a line of condoms. Instead of using their well-known label, however, the company is going to market them under the brand name "Hello Pussy."

The Attraction

"Hello, my name is _____; how do you like me so far?"
—Voted by *Cosmo* readers as pick-up line most likely to succeed

Transitioning from an exclusive to a more inclusive form of intimate relationship is not for everybody. Only a small percentage of all couples are interested in making this shift. Involving others intimately in their erotic/romantic activities seems to appeal mainly to couples with certain needs and motivations.

The possibility of exploring consensual intimate involvements with outsiders appears to be of interest primarily to couples that already have a strong bond with each other and are secure in their own relationship. Those that are not secure in their bonding may be too involved in resolving issues between themselves to consider taking on new and potentially disruptive challenges.

In addition, couples that have good communication between the partners and in which each is sensitive to the needs of the other seem to be more attracted to exploring non-exclusive alternatives. Conversely, non-possessive arrangements do not generally hold much attraction for the partners of couples who are insensitive to and/or uncommunicative with each other.

Transitioning to non-possessiveness may appeal to couples that are experiencing certain unresolved needs. Common situations in which a lack of something in the relationship is strongly felt may occur when:

- one or both partners feel that the sexual/romantic excitement in their union is waning and they are looking for ways to enhance their intimacy together.
- one partner has a much higher sex drive than the other partner and the couple is looking together for a way to relieve the stress of this imbalance on both partners.
- one or both partners have a strong need to have sex outside of their relationship but they don't want to lie about it or cheat on their partner.
- one or both partners do not want to have control restrictions placed on them by their partner but want to be free to explore their sexuality spontaneously, without guilt.

By restructuring the terms of their arrangement to include at least some elements of erotic non-possessiveness, the couple may hope to satisfy some of these needs and resolve some of the underlying tensions before they become a source of significant conflict.

A major appeal of the shift toward involving others intimately is that it most often occurs as an adaptive, problem-solving strategy, evolved jointly by the partners of the couple, to improve their relationship.

Going non-possessive can be appealing to individuals and couples for less salutary reasons, however. One partner in a couple may prompt this shift deceptively as a way to dissolve the current relationship and look for a new primary partner. A couple close to breaking up may try swinging, for example, as a last resort to save their relationship.

There appear to be at least a few of these maladaptive couples in any given social setting involving intimate non-possessive activities. For the most part, their relationships tend to be unstable, the partners drift apart, and they do not continue with this type of lifestyle.

Such individuals can be perceived as problematic, however, by the majority of more stable couples that are involved in non-possessive communities. Persons seen as emotionally needful may be disruptive to the playfulness ethic and may attempt to intrude themselves into existing relationships. As such, they are often regarded with caution.

An amusing twist on a classic scenario can be observed in this context. In the traditional world, a young woman might be given advice such as, "Watch out for Chuck. He's not looking to marry someone; he just wants to have sex with you." At a recreational sex event, the advice might be, "Watch out for Chuck. He doesn't just want to just have sex with you; he's looking for someone to marry."

CHAPTER SIX

Swinging and "The Lifestyle"

Swinging is generally understood as the practice of couples getting together to exchange partners for the purpose of having sex. Couples who swing represent one of the many varieties of non-possessive intimate relationships. Swinging is almost entirely a couples-only scene and is by far the most common way for those who are married to engage in consensual non-monogamous activities.

Webster's defines "to swing" as "to be ultra-fashionable, especially in seeking pleasure" or "to engage in casual sexual relations."[1] No one seems to be quite sure how the term "swinging" became the original label of choice to describe this spouse-swapping practice but some associations with the word can offer suggestions.

To be a swinger has had positive connotations since at least the jazz age of the 1920s. The obvious connection with being hip, sophisticated, and avant-garde was likely a factor in the adoption of swinging as a self-description among those who first explored consensual non-possessive arrangements. Also relevant was the implied sense of rhythm and oscillation back and forth between alternative positions.

Whatever its origins, "swinging" became the code word used by couples in the 1970s and '80s to describe their covert (from the outside world) mate-trading activities. While an improvement over the sexist "wife-swapping" designation of the 1960s, the term, "swinging" is now considered somewhat dated by most participants. As the decades of the 1990s and the aughts unfolded, couples who shared other couple's partners for sex began to refer to themselves as being in "the lifestyle."[2]

Again, we see a relatively innocuous and somewhat generic term used a code word to signal membership in a covert subculture. As is the case with most slang, coded terms such as swinging, have a limited life trajectory.

Typically, some in-group coins a new word or phrase which gains credence among the limited number of group members who are closely involved. At some point, the new term may be picked up by the popular media and used to characterize the activities of these individuals who may be seen as deviant in some way.

As the term gains widespread acceptance in the mainstream culture, it loses its cachet as a secret code reference. Some other new term is then coined by the insiders to replace it and the cycle begins again.

Although mate-swapping for sex has probably existed since the dawn of time, this type of activity never gained any significant traction until the late 1960s and early 1970s. The advent of the birth-control pill, the empowerment of women, and the seismic shift in Western culture toward a challenging of the repressive values of the previous generation all created a kind of perfect storm of sexual relationship experimentation.

The popular media hyped these experiments to the mainstream audience with sensationalized accounts of the Sexual Freedom League on campus, group marriages in the communes. and "key parties" in the suburbs.

The 1980s and '90s saw the rise and proliferation of swing clubs designed to provide safe and comfortable venues for couples to meet and engage in non-commercial recreational sex. More recently, as with so many other aspects of contemporary interaction, the Internet has emerged as a primary vehicle for social networking among those couples looking to hook-up with like-minded others.

Since its early beginnings a few decades ago, swinging has grown tremendously in popularity and now the "lifestyle" constitutes a full-fledged social movement and cultural phenomenon. Although still somewhat below the radar of mainstream society, those involved in this style of relationship probably now number in the millions; active clusters of participants can be found in virtually every population center, especially in North America and Europe.

Swinging takes place somewhat differently in several different contexts. One of the best ways to get a feel for what actually happens in this notoriously covert sub-culture is to examine the various venues devoted to lifestyle activities.

Recreational Sex Clubs

"'Curiouser and curiouser!' cried Alice."[3]

—Lewis Carroll

Most mainstream people are relatively unaware that there are places (a lot of them!) where you can go to have non-commercial sex with others seeking the same thing. Occasionally, conflicts with local authorities may be reported in the media but, generally, these "rec sex" clubs remain unobtrusive and part of an underground network known only to couples and singles involved in this type of activity.

Although the origins of these "on-premises" clubs are a bit unclear, some of the first to be established were "Plato's Retreat" in New York City during the 1970s (see the documentary *American Swing*[4]) and similar venues in Los Angeles in the 1980s.

Since then, the number of these clubs has increased dramatically with at least one now present in almost every city and town of any size. The National Association of Swing Clubs of America (NASCA), the largest trade association, now lists several hundred member clubs in their directory.[5]

These clubs, with names like Trapeze, Club Colette, and New Horizons, may take many different forms but almost all include at least one socializing area and one "play" area. Often resembling a typical nightclub, the socializing area may have cabaret-style seating with a bar, buffet food, dance floor, and so on. Where the recreational sex clubs are radically different from traditional nightclubs, however, is in the addition of the play rooms.

Often located upstairs or in an annex to the socializing area, the play area is frequently divided up into several spaces designed for erotic activity. Spaces may range from the utilitarian to the fanciful but most will have padded platform beds or padded mats on the floor. A free supply of condoms, lubricants, and tissues is usually provided.

Some play rooms have doors that can be closed or even latched for privacy. Most, however, are at least partially open to view (often through peepholes) or have an entrance covered only by a curtain.

In addition to the smaller spaces suitable for one couple only, there are usually spaces that can accommodate two couples together and often larger "orgy rooms" for group activity. Some clubs also offer specialized rooms providing, for example, equipment for bondage activities or "dark rooms" for anonymous encounters.

The play rooms are often arrayed along both sides of a central walkway, allowing members the opportunity to stroll along to observe participants in action and to select the space they prefer for their own activities. Interactions between and among couples frequently occur as people are passing each other while cruising along these promenades. A look, a word, a touch, and strangers may become intimate friends, at least temporarily.

A typical evening's schedule at "The Pendulum Club" will start with members arriving dressed in nightclub clothes, although the women may be attired in more provocative outfits than would ordinarily be acceptable at a mainstream club. The early phase of the evening usually consists of attendees eating, drinking, socializing, and dancing. So far, there is not much happening that is significantly different from the ordinary activities seen in any other nightclub.

The careful observer may notice, however, that the dancing is more erotic, there is a lot of overt touching and fondling going on, and people are talking and dancing with people other than the ones with whom they came. This is somewhat of a contrast to the traditional couple-oriented dance clubs in which the partners of a couple "behave themselves" in public and stay pretty much exclusively with each other.

Also, in recreational sex club socializing/dancing activities, there is relatively little expression of jealousy seen on the part of one partner when the other partner is openly flirting with or attempting to seduce attractive prospects. This, again, is in stark contrast to the possessiveness seen in traditional nightclubs where each person often guards their partner closely to prevent against incursions by others who may be viewed as competitors.

The real difference from an ordinary nightclub, however, emerges when people in a recreational sex club start moving from the socializing area to the play rooms.

Sometimes, this transition begins with an announcement or the playing of a specific song as a signal. (Go to Fun4Two in the Netherlands and watch what happens when the DJ plays their theme song, "Take Your Clothes Off.") Often, however, it's just a spontaneous migration as people feel the mood is right to get down to the business of why they're there.

Frequently, at this point, there is a costume change as women may shed their outer garments and slip into their sexiest lingerie. Tapping into the vast market for specialized "club wear," many women use the opportunity to wear what they may not dare anywhere else.

Function trumps fashion in this setting, however, and although everybody wants to look hot, women learn that outfits with elaborate fasteners, etc., are too much of a nuisance to get out of when the occasion arises. Instead of fetish wear items, such as tight leather or vinyl outfits, most women opt for maximizing accessibility and convenience. (Crotchless panties are very popular.)

Men, being naturally more functional, may simply strip down to boxers or just wrap a towel around their waist and go commando.

One of the shocking eye-openers (literally) for newcomers is the common "co-ed" locker rooms with both genders disrobing in full view and close proximity to each other. This titillation (!) is, of course, mild in terms of what's to come.

Once they are dressed for success, the participants may promenade around the passageways looking in, where possible, to the play rooms to see who is doing what with whom. Cruising the play area and looking for opportunities to engage with others is the primary activity of this latter part of the evening.

Due at least in part to (usually male) stamina limitations, most couples will alternate playroom sessions with R&R periods in the bar or dance area. Once recovered, it's back into the fray for more hunting and gathering. Eventually, but often not before the early morning hours, couples start changing back into their street clothes and heading home.

Hooking-Up Patterns

"How do I love thee? Let me count the ways."[6]
—Elizabeth Barrett Browning

Couples vary greatly in terms of how involved they become at a recreational sex club. Personal preferences, anxieties, the attractiveness of other couples, and the perceived ambience of the setting can all interact to modulate comfort level. Based on factors such as these, at least four types of engagement patterns can be identified at rec sex clubs.

At the most limited end of the range, some couples never leave the socialization area preferring to stop with just the stimulation provided there. The partners of the couple may go home by themselves and have enhanced sex with each other as a result of experiencing the erotically-charged atmosphere of the club.

Some couples wander the play areas but only as voyeurs, watching but not engaging physically with others. They may use the club as a sort of "live porn" viewing opportunity to stimulate their own arousal for when they get back home.

Many couples use the play area to have sex but only by themselves as a couple and do not engage with others. They may choose a secluded spot or, if they are more adventuresome, may "perform" in an area visible to voyeurs. The awareness of being watched by others may, perhaps, add excitement not generally available in their otherwise routine sexual interactions.

Most couples, however, use the play rooms to have sex with other couples. For these people, having an erotic connection with someone other than your primary partner is the main purpose of the recreational sex club experience. Again, for this, the largest group, several patterns can be identified.

Some participants come to the club as part of a foursome or larger group of people, all of whom have had sex with each other previously. For these paired couples or groupies, it's a simple matter of finding a suitable play space and getting it on with each other in familiar combinations.

Most couples, however, arrive as independents and are in search mode, looking for others with whom to connect. How these hook-ups occur and the subtle and not so subtle seductions that take place between and among couples are complex and interesting enough to warrant a separate treatise on this topic. (Further research is clearly needed here!)

For now, suffice it to say that just as singles in the traditional dating rituals flirt, seduce, and engage, so do couples in the rec sex environment, with the important distinction that generally, not just two but four people need to agree before any consummation occurs.

Regular attendees at a particular club will almost certainly encounter other members with whom they have connected previously, and these may provide familiar opportunities for a repeat performance. More exciting, however, may be the chance to encounter fresh prospects and to make intimate with heretofore strangers.

Many of the interactions are fleeting and one-time encounters. As couples engage repetitively over time with other couples, however, the relationships that are formed can be very strong and long lasting. Some couples report that the people they play with are their very best friends and they share intimacies with them that go much beyond the purely physical.

Seduction

"Seduction isn't making someone do what they don't want to do;
Seduction is enticing someone into doing what they secretly want to
do already."[7]

—Benjamin Russell

As compared to the oftentimes lengthy courtship rituals in the traditional singles scene, seduction between couples in the rec sex playrooms is generally very streamlined. Everybody knows what everybody is there for and the question essentially comes down to, "Do you want to do it with us now or with some other couple later?"

"Seduction," if it even can be called that, can be very rapid and entirely nonverbal. At times, even between strangers, just a first look or a touch can lead directly into very brief foreplay and immediate penetration.

The concept of seduction, by most definitions of the term, generally involves some notion of somebody leading someone else astray. In the rec sex context, at least among experienced participants however, few people could be considered to be persuaded to engage in activities they wouldn't engage in otherwise.

In these venues, seduction is more focused on the who rather than the what. People attempt to persuade those they find attractive to do the familiar activity with them rather than somebody else.

Successful seduction essentially involves persuading a reluctant possibility to move from a state of unwillingness to one of acceptance. In many ways, this process proceeds much like it does in the well-known singles dating scene, with some notable exceptions.

Most significantly, with four people often involved, seduction can get a bit complex. In the most common scenario, the male of each couple will attempt to prompt willingness on the part of the female of the other couple.

Two couples meeting each other, possibly as first-time prospects, will often initially switch partners for a hug and a brief caress to assess the mutual level of interest in proceeding. Adjourning to a nearby sofa, perhaps, there may be side-by-side seduction attempts unfolding.

Typically, each female will make an independent decision as to whether to take matters to the next level with her prospective suitor. She will most probably be keeping an eye on her primary partner's progress with his prospect, however. Her decision to proceed or not may be influenced, one way or the other, by her assessment of how likely his liaison is to occur.

There will be one of three outcomes from these parallel seductions. In the most straightforward result, both females may make a go or no-go choice congruently, with appropriate actions following. Then there are the split decisions.

When one of the newly-paired playmates wants to get it on and the other does not, further decisions need to be made. Some primary-partner couples only "play together," meaning that it has to be a go for both or it doesn't happen. Others are comfortable allowing each primary partner to play independently.

In the case of the independence-agreement couples, the one pair who wanted to do each other would go off and find an appropriate place to get physical while the other pair might go to the bar or dance floor and simply socialize until their primary partners returned. ("Do you think our spouses are having a good time together?")

In an advanced level of play, the leftover couple might decide to go off together and attempt to find others to seduce that might be more to their liking. Among experienced participants, creative decisions like these are handled with a nonchalance that would be shocking to those unfamiliar with this lifestyle.

With no need to engage in prolonged and complex mating dances, many participants find the rec sex experience to be refreshingly direct and honest. Freed from the game-playing and deceptiveness so prevalent in the monogamous pick-up bar scene, lifestyle people value assertive expression and uninhibited fulfillment of their sexual desires and needs.

As part of this ethic, seduction is recognized and valued as an important aspect of erotic expression and one that can be developed to a high level of skill and sophistication. Just as with S&M participants, both seducer and seducee enjoy their roles and each typically attempts to heighten the intensity of their dance together.

Although, as in the mainstream world, men usually take the lead role in initiating sexual proposals, in the rec sex environment, women can be equal-opportunity seducers. Many women report a feeling of exhilaration that comes with the freedom, perhaps for the first time, of seeing an attractive man and approaching him with a straight-forward invitation to have sex. Some women liken this freedom to Erica Jong's concept of the "zipless fuck." (Read *Fear of Flying*.[8])

Both men and women in the non-possessive lifestyle see this environment as offering an erotic wish fulfillment opportunity that can be free from guilt, jealousy, possessiveness, power manipulations, deception, gender inequality, and other negative emotions and behaviors so common in sexual activities in the monogamous world.

Seduction often gets a bad rap in the mainstream world. The classic image of the Lothario leading the innocent maiden astray is universally regarded as an example of immorality. In the non-possessive scene, however, seduction is often viewed as a joyful dance in which both parties participate voluntarily and work together to heighten the erotic potential of the pas de deux.

Seduction can, of course, occur any time, any place. Seating arrangements at a group table with many people, for example, are often scrutinized for their seduction possibilities. Choosing to sit next to an attractive person you want to meet can lead to seductive opportunities.

He: (while stroking her leg under the table) So, how many glasses of wine would it take for you to want to have sex with me?

She: Oh, I don't know. Why don't you pour me another one and let's find out.

Consumer Satisfaction

"The customer is always right."[9]

—César Ritz

"The customer always comes first!"

—Heidi Fleiss

Rec sex clubs have been a growth industry recently because, like all successful businesses, they have evolved, often through trial and error, to meet the needs of their customers.

Although the early clubs were quite limited and unimaginative in their operations (and some still are), most of the modern venues have now morphed into quite sophisticated facilities. Catering to a target demographic of mostly affluent business/professional people, these clubs have learned how to provide a controlled environment where members feel safe to indulge in their sexuality, while exploring the boundaries of how uninhibited they are comfortable being.

Mostly urban in location, some of these facilities are very impressive with thousands of square feet of floor space, high-tech DJ equipment, gourmet food, immaculately clean play areas, and well-trained staff to provide comfort and security for their clientele. These amenities do come with a price, however, with the fee for a single visit often exceeding $100 per couple.

Rec sex clubs have prospered also because they have operationalized a fundamental principle of how consensual non-possessive sex works. Specifically, they understand that although the males will almost always be lustful, for any extra-couple intimacies to occur, the females involved need make the go/no-go decision. This tenet is often humorously expressed as, "Men may drool but women rule."

Successful rec sex clubs have implemented this principle in many ways to make women members feel secure and empowered. All of these clubs have house rules, for example, which those entering must agree to abide. Many of these regulations are specifically designed to enhance the comfort level of the female members.

One way in which female sensibilities are supported is in the virtually universal mantra of "No means no," which is a part of the rules of almost every club. This statement essentially codifies the woman's prerogative to choose her own sex partners and to be free from coercion, whether verbal or physical, by eager males. Men who do not respect a woman's right to choose will find themselves subject to the club's sanctions, including expulsion.

Another female-sensitive restriction is the common rule of no touching unless permission is requested and granted. Clubs without this restriction may have to respond to sexual-harassment type complaints from women exposed to unwanted groping by strangers.

Rec sex clubs protect women's sensitivities also by limiting the browsing activities of the male members. There is often a prohibition on men cruising the play areas alone, for example. Many clubs require men to be accompanied by a female companion when looking for opportunities to engage.

In the rec sex environment, most women feel more comfortable in engaging with a new man if he comes already attached to another female. Single men, if admitted at all, may be identified by a wristband and restricted to the socialization area unless invited specifically by a female to accompany her to the play rooms.

Women are generally more skittish than men regarding images of themselves being recorded when they are involved in what might be considered compromising situations. As a result, virtually all rec sex clubs prohibit any type of photography.

Because so many devices now have imaging capabilities, many clubs require everyone to turn in their mobile phones and tablets at the entrance. (One participant commented that this policy is reminiscent of the code of the Wild West where everyone had to check their guns at the door before entering the saloon.)

New applicants for admission are screened at the door to eliminate any potential undesirables, such as those who may appear overly aggressive, drunk, poorly dressed, and so on. Roving staff members inside monitor activities to enforce rules and provide assistance, if there are complaints. The end result is much like an adult version of the kindergarten teacher's wish, where everyone plays nicely with each other.

The emphasis on distaff priorities may seem a bit sexist but it pays off for all concerned. Women who can relax and feel empowered are more likely to be responsive to invitations to play and more likely to return to this venue, tell their girlfriends to come, etc.

The observation that focusing on female comfort levels is good also for the guys and the club owners is expressed in the commonly-heard saying that, "If the women are happy, everybody's happy."

Singles with Couples: Pros and Cons

"The only really happy people are married women and single men."[10]

—H. L. Mencken

Single males and females who want to connect with existing couples often seek opportunities by scrolling through the myriad of websites devoted to this type of arrangement. Alternatively, singles may also attempt to hook up with couples by attending recreational sex clubs, resorts, cruises, and more. In these venues, they may encounter a form of (reverse) sexism.

Although generally geared toward a couples-membership priority, many rec sex clubs and events do admit singles, usually on some limited basis. Single women are almost always welcomed and often offered free entry or discounted admission fees. Single males, however, may be prohibited entirely as members or, if allowed at all, may be carefully restricted to reflect the preferences of women which, of course, can be quite complex.

The advantages of providing incentives to attract single women to rec sex venues are obvious and similar to the "ladies' night" promotion at traditional bars. Single women are perceived by club owners and event promoters as an added attraction to the (mainly) coupled men and their presence is considered likely to boost attendance.

Single women who attend rec sex events are often called "unicorns." Although some have suggested that this is because they are so rare as to be mythical creatures, the reality is that, in virtually any lifestyle event of any size, there are likely to be at least a few unattached females. (Perhaps a better reason for the unicorn label is that these women are perceived as being both single and horny.)

Many unicorns are bisexual and, as such, have something to offer both partners of a couple. As such, they are highly valued and may find themselves the recipient of seduction initiatives by both members of a couple.

Whereas single women are usually given preferential treatment (free drinks, amenities, etc.) at many rec sex establishments, single men, however, face significant obstacles in even gaining entry to these clubs. They may have to pay much higher fees, be allowed in only on a quota system, or, most frequently, not be admitted at all.

This double standard appears to reflect the different threat potential of single males versus that of single females, as perceived by the partners in the couples who are the primary customers at these venues.

Both the male and female partners of a couple at a rec sex event typically view the presence of single females as a positive. For the male, it's one more sexual possibility and one for which he may not even have to trade off his own female.

The female of the couple generally does not regard single females as threatening and, in fact, often perceives them as a good thing in several ways, such as:

- a way to "outsource" her sexual obligation to her male partner without having to engage with a strange guy as part of a swap arrangement
- a way to distract her male partner while she seeks attention from other men and an additional possibility for a girl-on-girl encounter.

The reactions of the partners of a couple to single men in the play areas are also complex but much more negative overall. The male of the couple may view the presence of single men as potentially threatening in that:

- single men may be viewed as unfair competition, especially if they are perceived to be (as is often the case) younger, better looking, or better sexual performers than the male partner
- single men who want to engage with his female partner may be resented as trying to get something for nothing because they have no partners of their own to trade.

Some female partners of a couple may also view the presence of single males in the play areas as threatening in that:

- single males may be seen as too aggressive and not respectful enough of a woman's right to decline offers
- single males may, at times, join together and be seen by women as prowling wolf packs, raising the threat of possible coercion (although this never seems to actually happen).

These concerns appear to reflect a common perception among many women that single males are less "civilized" because they lack the moderating influence of a female partner. (Perhaps as a result of this sexist attitude, some women attempt to "cure" single men of this deficiency by persuading them to bond into a relationship with them.)

At the other end of the attitude continuum, however, both partners of a couple often see the benefits of single-male availability at rec sex clubs and events. The most obvious positive is the possibility of connecting with an attractive single male to "double-team" the female partner for the enjoyment of all three players.

A male partner of a couple may view single males as a gift for his female partner and may encourage her to enjoy them as an expression of his generosity. In a similar vein, some male partners may derive sexual excitement from offering their female partners to single males as a sort of "pimp my wife" scenario.

Additionally, some male partners, who may have difficulty performing themselves, may simply enjoy watching their female partner in action with a single male, without having for himself any obligation to satisfy any other female. This type of outsourcing thus may serve to meet the needs of both members of the couple.

Many of the more adventuresome female partners of couples may also see several obvious advantages to having single males added to a couples' play environment. The additional single males provide a larger pool of "talent" from which the female partners may draw, especially when they may be selected for youth, good looks, performance skills, and so on.

Also, given the physiological limitations of males after one or more ejaculations, the availability of additional single males provides, for the female partner, an opportunity to continue seeking sexual satisfaction with fresh troops. ("Don't give up hope, Virginia, reinforcements are on the way." [Play the bugle charge fanfare here.])

Singles with Couples: Policies and Procedures

"The only really happy people are married women and single men."[11]
—H. L. Mencken

"Yes, this is true, especially when the two of them get together!"
—Anonymous

Clearly, the issue of allowing singles, especially males, into rec sex venues is a complex one with many positive and negative viewpoints possible. Operators of clubs, resorts, cruises, etc., attempt to balance these perspectives as they create their policies regarding admission of the unattached.

The majority of couples participating in rec sex activities appear to prefer a couples-only policy. There is a sizeable minority, however, who are either tolerant of or who actually prefer some single-male availability.

Reconciling these somewhat opposing preferences creates a bit of a quandary for those who organize these activity settings.

In the rec sex business world, the single-male "market" is huge and unattached men are willing to pay higher admission prices, creating a potentially lucrative opportunity for venue operators. Opening the doors to too many or the wrong type of single men can drive away the club's primary resource of couples, however.

The early clubs opened admission to anyone with no gender restrictions and this policy, perhaps predictably, resulted in male/female ratios often exceeding 10:1. The few females who first visited these clubs often felt like deer in a den of wolves and did not return. Realizing that their survival depended upon attracting women as actively participating members, the operators of rec sex clubs and events started to explore ways to limit gender ratios, leading to the development of several strategies.

The most common approach is a strict couples-only policy and many clubs prohibit single males under any circumstances. Many women feel most comfortable in the rec sex environment when potential sex partners come already attached to another woman. A man accompanied by his wife/girlfriend is generally perceived as not only more likely to be better behaved but is easier to dismiss afterwards with less likelihood of unwanted follow-up or other complications.

Some clubs may limit the number of single males to the number of single females admitted, thus preserving gender balance. Some clubs allow larger male/female admission ratios, such as 2:1 or 3:1, often on specific nights. Others may prohibit single males until after midnight, for example.

Other alternatives to the single-male admission problem include the following creative solutions that are usually scheduled as special events:

- "trio nights" in which threesomes of two males and one female are allowed to be admitted (frequently resulting in much pleading by single men waiting outside as couples arrive)
- "gigolo nights" in which the club invites specific single males valued by women for their attractiveness and sexual skillfulness, identifies them with some symbol, such as a bow-tie, and makes them available on demand to women
- "idol nights" in which hopeful single men dance briefly on stage and are voted in or out for that night by the women present.

Some clubs do not restrict gender ratios at all and count on attracting those women for whom a large selection of male talent is desirable. Somewhat popular also are those events, often marketed as "gang-bang" nights, which may attract women with high-level sexual needs and large numbers of eager men.

The Newbie Experience

"There is no aphrodisiac like innocence."[12]

—Jean Baudrillard

Almost everyone now involved in consensual non-possessive intimate activities started at some time to explore what it would be like to expand the boundaries of an exclusive relationship. Their curiosity piqued perhaps by media titillations, such as the short-lived television series *Swingtown*,[13] a couple may decide to check out the possibilities for themselves.

This initial exploration may take many forms, such as visiting online sites for couples dating or expressing interest to other couples they know who may already be involved in this activity. For many inexperienced couples, however, a defining moment of their entry into the non-possessive lifestyle is their first visit to a recreational sex club.

This event often becomes a kind of loss of virginity for the couple's heretofore sexual exclusivity and, like other similar rites of passage, becomes an experience that may be extensively discussed and long remembered.

The first visit to a rec sex club is usually also fraught with strong emotions, running through a whole gamut of anxieties and excitement. These intense feelings typically are a result of information underload, as the couple struggle to cope with all the what-ifs from a perspective of knowing very little about what generally happens in these situations.

The many choices confronting each of the partners of the couple are often viewed as approach/avoidance conflict scenarios, meaning, they are both attracted to and fearful of what might happen. The partners typically engage in a kind of risk/reward, cost/benefit analysis as they make go/no-go decisions at each step in the process.

The initial foray into a rec sex event is most often prompted by the male partner and agreed to cautiously by the female partner. Although the male partner may be driven to explore a club by lustful fantasies, he may also be concerned about his performance ability in this new, possibly on-demand environment.

The male partner may also be concerned about how he will react when his honey is responding passionately to the advances of another guy. ("Will I be jealous, excited, aroused, fascinated, or all of the above?")

The female partner may be attracted by curiosity but concerned about her appearance, especially without some or all of her usual supports (such as clothing!). She may have conflicting anxieties (and/or wishes!).

On the one hand, she may worry that she may not be perceived as attractive enough to elicit interest by other men. At the same time, she may worry that she will have to fend off large numbers of aroused males.

Both partners, whose previous experience may have only been behind closed doors, may experience trepidation regarding the possibility of having sex in view of others or even viewing others in the act. Although most new couples will have already watched enough porn to be familiar with how others do it, seeing it live for the first time, however, and especially up close and personal, can be both highly stimulating and even shocking for some people.

An additional anxiety/desire issue for some first-time men is the possibility of experiencing some homoerotic feelings upon seeing, maybe for the first time, other men in an aroused state. Women generally experience much less concern regarding the possibility of feeling attracted to other women and may view the rec sex club visit as an opportunity to explore this option.

As the new couple gets more comfortable with rec sex activities, they may find themselves more relaxed in responding to invitations from other couples. (After all, it's just sex.) They may even feel comfortable enough to try initiating play with others whom they find attractive.

Over time, the former beginner couple may find they have made a lot of new friends and these definitely come with fringe benefits! Many experienced rec sex couples have a whole social network of others with whom they have sex more or less frequently. So, instead of calling up the neighbors to see if they want to come over and play bridge, the couple might call them up to see if they want to come over to just play.

Orientation

"Welcome to the Fun House."[14]

—Jack Corbett

Recognizing the myriad anxieties and misperceptions that may preclude first-timers from becoming repeat customers, most rec sex clubs offer them various special accommodations. Virtually all clubs provide, and many require, a new member orientation session in which the club rules of conduct are explained, a Vegas-style agreement is signed (meaning, what happens at the club stays at the club), questions are answered, and, of course, fees are collected.

Many clubs have well-designed websites that may offer a virtual tour of the facilities before the new visitors even arrive. Of special interest to those new to these settings, these sites frequently provide an extensive FAQ section to address the most common queries.

When the first-timers arrive for their orientation, experienced members will often volunteer as guides to take the newbies on a tour of the socializing and play areas and answer further questions. Not totally altruistic, the old hands will be sizing up the newcomers as possible play partners and may graciously offer to assist them in losing their rec sex club virginity.

Misperceptions on the part of first-timers often involve demand expectations. Some newcomers may believe that once they enter a rec sex club, they will be required to have sex with anyone who requests it. Virtually all club's guidelines, therefore, stress that nobody needs to do anything they don't want to do.

Once the anxieties over external pressures are relieved somewhat, the newcomers are free to deal with the anxieties caused by internal insights, such as the possible realization that, OMG, I really *do* want to have sex with anyone who requests it! Such revelations may lead to some reorganization of self-concepts and may result in some redefinition on the part of the individual or the couple as to who they really are.

Orientation staff may suggest to nervous newbies that it is perfectly OK to just be voyeurs on their first visit and that, although there may be invitations, there is never any obligation to accept. Some clubs may schedule special nights for new members or designate special areas for those new to this type of environment. In these "beginner play areas," new couples may feel more at ease among those who share their uncertainties.

Some clubs may request or require that newcomers to this lifestyle indicate that they are novices, such as by wearing a special color lanyard. As a couple's status as beginners is discovered by other members, however, this may create the perhaps unintended effect of increasing the number of invitations to play, as experienced couples are often eager to "help" them lose their newbie designation. Somewhat akin to virgins on a college campus, the new couples may find themselves to be highly prized objects of attention.

A few rec sex clubs have evolved somewhat complex systems of identification of status and/or preferred/prohibited behaviors. In one common model, participants when arriving may choose from different colored wristbands, which may indicate things such as, blue=soft swap only, pink=bi-curious, black=S&M, and so on.

While helpful as signaling devices, systems that are too elaborate can have unintended consequences, however. One might observe, for example, an eager male who, while caressing a newfound female prospect with one hand may be thumbing through the code book with the other hand to see what is permitted/expected next.

It should be noted that rec sex clubs vary greatly in the amount and type of support they provide to prospective new members. Some function much like lifestyle incubators, investing considerable effort to ensure that new couples feel comfortable with their initial experiences.

Others take much more of a sink-or-swim approach. This laissez-faire style can be seen most commonly in the European clubs where, with typical continental attitude, it is assumed that anyone who would come to a rec sex club should already know how to behave and that it would be demeaning to try to teach sophisticated adults anything about sex. New couples, who may need a lot of hand holding at first, often begin with the North American clubs and then graduate to the European clubs for more advanced training.

Resorts

"For a while we pondered whether to take a vacation or get a divorce. We decided that a vacation is over in two weeks but a divorce is something you always have."[15]

—Woody Allen

In addition to the clubs primarily located in North American and European cities, there are a growing number of recreational sex resorts, mostly located in the Caribbean, Mexico, and around the Mediterranean. These vacation venues offer much the same activities as the mostly urban rec sex clubs but provide socializing and play opportunities in a warmer setting, often with an emphasis on outdoor frolicking.

"Lifestyle" resorts offer an alternative for those wanting an activity-based holiday. Instead of vacationing at a golf or ski resort, couples may choose to travel to a place where sex is the main recreational activity.

Couples typically book in about a week's stay at one of these exotic/erotic resorts. Offering an experience beyond the usual single-night activities at the temperate zone clubs, these extended stays provide a sort of immersion experience in the non-possessive lifestyle. Every day may offer new opportunities for hooking up (figuratively and literally) with others.

Because most city clubs are only open one or two nights a week, many encounters there may be one-night-stands. At the resorts, couples may find themselves engaging in repeated encounters night after night, with others they especially enjoy. These frequent liaisons, at times, develop into longer-term relationships, continuing after the couples have returned home.

A relatively new phenomenon in the lifestyle vacation planning industry has been the emergence of the rec sex cruise. Sort of like floating resorts, cruise ships offer intriguing possibilities for couples who like to play with each other.

These cruises can be organized on smaller river boats or on the largest of the ocean liners. Enthusiasts think of them as a sort of hard-core version of the *Love Boat* concept.

Offering the perception of total freedom from land-based restrictions and promoting their "romance of the sea" images, these cruises have seen an explosive growth in popularity in the last few years with some attracting thousands of participants. Similar to the resorts, the most popular variants have been those offering a total "take-over" of the ship, ensuring that everyone on board is, in fact, on board with the purpose of the cruise.

There are now several rec sex tour and travel companies that organize dozens of these specialty trips every year. With names like "Dream Pleasure Tours," "Luxury Lifestyle Vacations," and "Sensual Sojourns," they cater to vacationing couples who want to have the freedom to engage sexually with each other openly at high-end resorts or on luxury cruise ships.

Although these vacation-style venues may create an impression that there will be sexual activity anytime, anyplace, they too have their limitations as to where "play" is permitted. Common restrictions include, for example, no nudity in the dining room and no sex with staff.

Otherwise, however, opportunities for encounters abound and many couples return from these types of active vacations "complaining" that they are exhausted by all the activity.

In contrast to the way "adult" sex tours are organized (primarily for single men) these erotic travel opportunities never involve commercial sex workers. In the world of rec sex travel, nobody pays anybody to have sex with them.

The tour operators simply provide the accommodations and market these events/locations to potential attendees who may be looking for other like-minded couples or individuals. When sex occurs between or among the travelers then, it's strictly a not-for-profit enterprise.

The most common destinations are those specialty resorts, with names like "Hedonism," "Desire," and "Spice," which cater primarily to the rec sex trade. (So far, at least, the Disney organization has not shown any interest in opening a similar theme park.)

Tour operators may also organize rec sex events at more traditional resorts, often booking the entire property over a weekend or longer. These hotel "take-overs" are quite popular in the rec sex community as they offer the possibility of a secure total environment where inhibitions, along with clothes, can be shed among one's peer group.

By excluding those outside the rec. sex subculture, these takeovers provide some guarantee against encountering your Aunt Edna or your boss(!) and having to explain why you're sitting in the hot tub, naked.

Nudity encounters with those from the vanilla world do occur at times and may be opportunities for mischief. Because many rec sex resorts share a stretch of only partially secluded beach with other more traditional resorts, visitors from these other resorts may wander by, either inadvertently or deliberately, to see what is going on.

In addition to tanning in the nude, the rec sex people may play the game of "let's scandalize the tourists" by pretending to spontaneously engage in sex just when outsiders are walking by. Predictably, about half of the passing visitors will shield their eyes and flee from this shocking sight while the other half will run to get their cameras.

CHAPTER SEVEN

Digital Double Dating

It's almost hard to remember what it was like only a couple of decades ago, before everyone was connected online and smartphone-enabled. The exponential rise of the Internet's influence in our lives has changed so many things, including how people hook-up for sex.

Nothing much has changed about the actual physical aspects of the resultant activity, of course, but the process of connecting with potential sex partners has evolved significantly. This change from the old ways, which were based on such limited information processing, is so dramatic that it warrants consideration as yet another type of sexual revolution.

Among those involved in non-possessive intimate relationships, the availability of Internet resources plus high-speed e-communication and image transmission options have radically redefined how couples and singles locate and interact with each other. Internet surfing, texting, sexting, tweeting, and so on have not only made it easier and quicker to find compatible others but have streamlined the mutual assessment process and facilitated the eventual face-to-face (or other position) encounter.

Social/Sexual Networking

"If you own a smartphone, you have a 24-7 singles bar in your pocket."[1]
—Aziz Ansari

Dating has evolved over the last several decades, especially among the younger generations, such as the Millennials. Whereas couples used to go on "traditional" dates alone together, dating, especially among Generation Y couples, is more group-centered now.

These younger individuals frequently start within a social nexus from which they may pair off with preferred partners for more secluded/intimate interactions and then return to the group, perhaps repeating the process with other partners.

Although dating practices are more socially rather than individually based now, the exclusivist trajectory is still relatively unchanged for the vast majority of dating couples. Even as two individuals may continue their group-centered social activities, they may restrict their intimate contacts to each other as they progressively define themselves as a committed couple.

For a small but significant percentage of the date-ready population, however, other types of dating relationships may be observed. In one variation, two individuals may meet and become increasingly bonded in terms of emotional loyalty but continue to maintain intimate physical relationships with others.

This type of non-exclusive relationship may persist even as the couple evolves their commitment into marriage. This pattern is somewhat common among those who are already involved in alternate intimate lifestyles, such as swinging or polyamory. Some who start early in adult life with these relationship variations may never have had a period of monogamy with anyone.

Social networking can easily segue into sexual networking as the power of e-communication is harnessed to identify, assess, and connect with prospective playmates of both genders. In most urban centers, there are now loosely-aligned clusters of 20- and 30-somethings whose raison d'etre is the opportunity for social/sexual contacts.

These clusters, made up of both individuals and dating couples, can be said to be sort of group relationships, in which the members mostly know one another or are friends of friends. The network participants usually share common values, such as the benefits of fluid intimate connections along with some degree of social and emotional support.

Most of these network members distinguish between a somewhat larger pool of contacts, with whom their interaction is only social, and a smaller collection, their "rotation," with whom they have (or would like to have) sexual interactions. The more enterprising members may even set up differing ringtones to signal the status of each type of incoming contact. (Lady Antebellum's "Need You Now"[2] is a popular choice.)

Web-Based Coupling

"Jack and Jill went up the hill
To fetch a pail of water."[3]

—Traditional English nursery rhyme

Many couples begin to explore possibilities for external erotic encounters by perusing some of the many Internet sites devoted to dating for those who are already partnered. Some of these websites are subsets of popular hook-up services for singles while a growing number are now specialized for couples only.

With domains like swinglifestyle.com, lifestylelounge.com, and kasidie.com, these sites focus on helping the inquisitive partners search and find, as efficiently as possible, a compatible pair or a single with whom to have sex. As such, they are quite distinctly different from matchmaking sites or those catering to people looking for a mate, or at least a long-term relationship.

As with other dating services, the couples' sites offer the partners opportunities to post information about themselves and to scan information about others. The descriptive information posted can range from the quite conservative to the extremely explicit, depending on the comfort level of the couple and the policies of the site.

In addition to the verbiage, most sites offer the option to post photos. Again, these may range from the discreet to the hardcore, as the couple chooses the level of intensity they want to reveal to others. Many sites now offer multiple levels of presentation, with the more X-rated accessible only after obtaining permission from the posting couple.

Most couples prefer some degree of anonymity when posting on a publicly-accessible site, so play-names are often used and faces, if shown at all, may be masked in some creative way. (Imagine the possibilities.)

Almost all couples' sites provide for dual profiles, one for him and one for her, on the same page. Like the singles' sites, these conjoint listings offer an exposure opportunity in which the couple can "market" themselves to potentially-interested others.

For inexperienced couples who are curious about the double-dating scene, these sites often provide their first foray into the possibilities of consensual extra-relationship sex. As such, the decision to sign up and post a profile on a site is usually a significant watershed event for the couple.

The process of creating a profile and selecting descriptive words and photos to display forces the couple to consider existential choices about who they really are and how they are going to present themselves. Often, significant negotiation may occur at this point as the male and female members of the couple may find they have quite different initial ideas about discretion versus explicitness and so on.

Similar decisions must be resolved by the couple regarding what they really want and how they are going to go about getting it. Virtually all sites allow the couple to specify what they are looking for—e.g., couples only, a female for a threesome, a big black male, etc.

Once the couple has agreed on how to present their joint profile and have uploaded it, the next step is usually to begin screening the inquiries that come in and to choose which to respond to. This phase also generally evokes significant discussion between the partners and prompts them again to refine what it is they are, and are not, looking for.

Again, there may be much negotiation and compromise between the partners as they seek to identify others who appear likely to meet both of their needs. Some couples may be able to make these decisions with little more effort than say, choosing a movie that both may like. Others, especially couples new to this process, may agonize over their initial choices and engage in complex decision-making strategies.

Many of those couples frequently find it difficult to identify another couple in which both the male and the female appear equally attractive to the female and the male of the couple wanting to respond. In this scenario, couples often develop creative trade-off strategies to resolve the dilemma. In the most common version, for example, they may agree that one of the partners gets to choose the other couple this time and the next time, the other partner makes the choice.

Often, one of the partners will want to choose another couple in which the opposite-gender member of the other couple is particularly attractive to them. At times, the same-gender member of the other couple may be especially unattractive to the other partner.

For example, Bob may want he and Carol to hook-up with Ted and Alice because he thinks Alice is really hot. Carol, however, may regard Ted as overweight and unappealing physically and may be repulsed by the thought of having sex with him.

If this liaison does, in fact, occur, it may be because:

a.   Carol may sacrifice her own sensitivities in the spirit of generosity and bonding with Bob. (This is often referred to as the "taking one for the team" sports metaphor.)

b.   Carol has negotiated first dibs on their next couple choice. (She may deliberately choose a couple in which the male is a hunk but the female is overweight and unattractive, as payback for Bob.)

Decision-making is a lot simpler, of course, in those situations in which the couple is only looking for an outside single. This may be, for example, a female for the couple to have a three-way "date" with or a well-endowed black male for the female partner to engage with while the male partner watches.

In all of these situations, the partners of the couple express not only their preferences but also their restrictions on the possible selections. Often, these limits are expressed via an agreement that gives each partner veto power over the choices of the other partner. ("You can choose whoever you want but it can't be anyone under 40 or anyone who looks better than me.")

Many couples report experiencing considerable excitement and stimulation just in perusing the profiles and photos of potential "playmates" and in imagining how it might be to engage with them. Some couples never go beyond this phase and participate only in a kind of fantasy role-playing exercise.

For those who do go on to make contact with others online, the process continues with more decision-making, negotiation, and refining of preferences and goals.

For most couples responding to inquiries from others, there is usually a back-and-forth exchange initially in which additional information and photos (often progressively more revealing) are exchanged. This "getting to know you" phase allows each couple to more carefully assess whether the other prospects are a desirable, or at least acceptable, choice for them.

At this stage, anonymity may be maintained via the couples' dating website features or by e-mail contact only. If compatibility looks likely for both couples, progressively more confidential channels of communication, such as text and voice numbers, may be revealed.

At any point, one or both couples may decide not to continue progressing toward an actual meeting. For new couples, this may occur as a "cold feet" reaction when anxiety rises faster than arousal.

For all couples, termination of the "discovery phase" may occur when information is revealed that has been agreed to previously to be an unacceptable feature. ("OMG, they're smokers!")

First Dates

"What is a date, really, but a job interview that lasts all night? The only difference is there aren't many job interviews where you'll wind up naked."[4]
—Jerry Seinfeld

For those couples that do continue to explore options with their new "pen pals," at some point a face-to-face rendezvous must be arranged. This typically occurs after there has been some interchange of information and photos and a consensus is reached by each person involved that the possibility of having sex with the opposite gender outsider is attractive enough to take the process to the next level.

Although these first meetings may take place at the home of one of the couples, more often they are scheduled at a public location, such as a bar or restaurant. The obvious advantage of a public meeting place is that one (or both) of the couples then has the option to leave gracefully if things do not appear to be progressing satisfactorily.

Disengagement at this stage is relatively common as the first face-to-face meeting can reveal information that was not evident in the communications up to that point. One of the reasons most commonly given for non-continuation is disappointment with the physical appearance of the other couple. ("That photo they posted must have been taken 20 years ago!")

Similar to the deceptions encountered on matchmaking sites for singles, some couples may embellish their descriptive information, or even their photos, in an attempt to appear more attractive. Seeing the others in person can cause a couple to re-think the wisdom of pursing a liaison.

Unlike singles' meet-ups, however, in the couples' first encounter, there are four decision makers involved. Both the male and the female members of each couple must at least tacitly agree to proceed for any intimacies to occur and any one of the four can usually veto continuation.

Assuming all parties are go for the mission, after the initial in-person screening, conversation over drinks or dinner generally continues with further "getting to know you" discovery. In addition to generic inquiries and disclosures, the discussion inevitably turns to the topic of sex.

Subtle and more overt questions regarding preferences, limits, and so on are asked and answered. Some of these queries may have been posed and responded to in previous communications but, at this time, clarifications and confirmations can be made.

A common topic of discussion is the matter of the ways in which each couple is comfortable in participating. For example, the most common question, "How do you two like to play?" usually asks whether the partners of the couple prefer to separate from each other and retreat behind closed doors, each with their new playmate, or whether the couple prefers to engage with all four people in the same room, or possibly the same bed, together.

Inexperienced couples often prefer separate locations, allowing each partner to focus solely on their new playmate. Some newbie couples may experience significant internal conflict during sexual activity with another couple when all four parties can be seen and heard.

Both men and women who are new at this activity report considerable distraction, confusion, and other strong feelings as they try to alternate between focusing on their new sex partner and trying to watch/hear what their spouse is doing with their new lover.

More experienced couples, however, often prefer the enhanced stimulation opportunities that arise when both couples are active in close proximity. In addition to the stimulating effects of observing another couple having sex nearby, having everyone in the same room allows for mix and match possibilities.

In advanced couples play, the two males might switch back and forth between servicing the two females. Alternatively, the two females might use a tag-team approach to pleasuring the males. (During the transitions, high-fives can frequently be observed in these situations.)

Having all four in the same play space also allows for homoerotic possibilities. Girl-on-girl action is very common while sexual contact between the men is generally quite rare and almost always would need to be pre-negotiated.

Other topics of prediscussion may include what orifices are (and are not!) available and under what conditions. For example, it may be agreed that oral sex is OK without protection but vaginal penetration will require a condom, and for anal, you must use a condom plus lube.

Many of these preliminary discussions take place very matter-of-factly among experienced couples (who have often just met) in much the same way that ordinary couples might discuss game matters with new bridge partners. At times, the conversation may proceed in short-hand code. (For example, "I like French, English, and German, but not Greek without grease.")

In addition to expressing preferences and limitations, the first meeting between couples is an opportunity for each partner to assess the erotic potential of their opposite-gender prospect in the other couple. Seductive and flirtatious behaviors frequently occur between the male of one couple and the female of the other.

Verbal suggestiveness can escalate into touching, fondling, and more intimate physical contact, limited only by the need for some restraint, if in a public place. At this stage, the couples will most likely move to a more private location, such as a hotel room or one of the couple's homes.

Not all initial encounters move so directly, of course. With some initial get-togethers, the couples may only agree to have a future meeting to continue the sizing-up process.

Throughout this process, each partner of each couple is not only assessing the possibilities but also likely communicating to their primary partner whether they are leaning toward a go or no-go decision.

Again, so as not to be too obvious to the others, some couples develop code words or otherwise innocuous nonverbal gestures to express their level of motivation to continue. (Hand signals used by sports referees to indicate infractions or success appear to be popular in this regard.)

One observer commented that while watching two newly-met couples, the interactions between each set of partners included so much ear pulling, nose rubbing, stomach patting, and the like that it reminded him of watching the third-base coach signal to the batter as to whether a hit-and-run play was on.

As an alternative to full-contact play, some couples may agree to have only limited interaction with their opposite numbers. For example, some couples may decide to switch partners but only for dancing and/or continued seduction/flirtation/fondling activities at this time.

Some, who may define themselves as "soft-swing" couples, never go beyond this type of titillation. They use the initial verbal and physical interaction with other couples as a way to stimulate arousal for intercourse, but only between themselves. Typically, the permitted interactions with others may include everything up to, but not including, penetration, which is reserved for their primary partner only.

Of course, soft-swing couples are expected to disclose this status before proceeding much beyond initial communication with other couples, the vast majority of which are looking for a more intromissive interaction. Failure to disclose this limitation may lead to the unsuspecting prospects being left with hard feelings (both figuratively and literally).

Private Parties

"The only rule is don't be boring and dress cute wherever you go. Life is too short to blend in."[5]

—Paris Hilton

Kind of part way between Internet dating for couples and on-premises recreational sex clubs are those hybrid events often called hotel parties. These are frequently set up by some kind of rec. sex membership organization that charges a fee for participation in the event.

"Couples-R-Us" may book a large suite at a local hotel and send out a notice, specifying when and where, to those on their e-mail contact list. (Many non-possessive couples maintain a separate e-mail address specifically for rec sex communications, thus avoiding embarrassing mix-ups in responding to invitations to attend the next meeting of the PTA.)

On the designated night, attendees may gather at the hotel bar for some drinks in a "meet and greet" format. At that time, new members can be introduced and those already familiar with each other can get reacquainted. (Hugs and kisses may ensue.)

If the reception is held at a location open to the general public, some discretion is necessary, especially in trying to determine who is, and who is not, part of the rec sex group. (Amusing misunderstandings may occur.)

If music is available, there may be an opportunity to try out potential new partners on the dance floor. Observations from this activity may be helpful in making choices later when there is an opportunity for a more intimate form of dancing.

At some appointed time, the attendees start making their way to the party rooms. To avoid interlopers, the organizers often prevent entry to those who are not authorized. ("Sorry, but we don't seem to have a 'Rob Lowe' on our guest list.") To avoid interruptions, entry may be restricted after a certain time point.

Socializing may continue upstairs but the participants are really there for some serious playtime and, before long, people start pairing up. Sort of like a more adult version of the high-school prom, the more popular attendees usually get things started first with those more hesitant remaining in the wallflower pool.

These events often involve a number of people in the relatively small space of a hotel suite. Because of space limitations, there may be limited options for privacy. ("We could do it in the bathroom.")

As a result, much of the sexual activity takes place in areas that may be visible to all. Surveying the suite packed with undulating bodies, one observer commented that it looked like a horizontal cocktail party.

Many couples report that they find it very stimulating to be having sex in an area where several other couples are also doing the same thing. Using the sights and sounds as stimulation for their own arousal, couples may find that they may have multiple opportunities for different types of engagement.

A few attendees may have minimal contact with others and may only be comfortable as voyeurs. Some primary partners, e.g., those of the soft-swing persuasion, may have sex only with each other, neither initiating nor accepting invitations from others. At the other end of the continuum, some couples operate like sexual butterflies, flitting from whoever is available now to whoever is available next.

The presence of several active couples also offers opportunities for group interaction. There is usually at least one large bed or one soft carpeted area in which several people may be pleasuring each other simultaneously in various combinations.

These clusters, sometimes called "puppy piles," probably represent the closest thing in the modern world to the ancient hedonistic rituals attributed to Bacchus and Dionysus.[6] Only a few of the attendees routinely participate in these orgiastic encounter groups, however. Most participants are more selective regarding their sex-partner choices and prefer one-on-one sessions with some kind of preliminaries and foreplay, however brief they may be.

House Parties

"A girl told me she never gets invited to parties. I told her, 'Just wear a short enough skirt and the party will come to you.'"[7]
—Dorothy Parker

"There's no place like home" might read the e-mailed invitation from a couple organizing a rec sex soiree at their place. These events play out much like hotel room parties but, if the house is large enough, they may allow for a greater number of participants. A spacious residence may also offer more options for those seeking secluded liaisons or more creative alternatives for sex in common areas (in the backyard, on the dining room table, and so on).

House parties often have themes in which the participants may come dressed in costumes of some kind. These, of course, get progressively discarded as the activity heats up.

Nevertheless, these themed events offer much in the way of erotic stimulation and creativity with opportunities to dress up as and sexualize a favorite mythical character. (The role of Snow White seems to be favored by women looking for multiple partners.)

House parties sometimes feature erotic games as ice-breakers and to encourage maximum interaction among attendees. Children's amusements, such as spin the bottle, can be morphed into adult versions. The musical chairs concept is another popular house party game that offers many possibilities to be tweaked for erotic potential.

As with all rec sex events, the primary purpose of these parties is to provide opportunities for couples to seek out other compatible couples or singles to assess and sample their erotic potential. Again, there is almost never any demand to participate, although there may be considerable attempts at persuasion, seduction, pleading, and so forth across both directions of the male-female divide.

One well-known house party game captured the national attention and achieved a kind of (sub)urban legend status several decades ago. The infamous "key parties" allegedly originating in the 1970s were picked up by the popular media and portrayed in many articles, books, and movies (see *The Ice Storm*[8]) as titillation for the general public.

As the story went, the male member of each couple arriving at these parties would drop his house keys into an opaque container. Upon leaving the party, each female member would, without looking, pick a set of keys out of the container. She would then go home with whomever's keys she got.

Ultimately then, everybody would be randomly paired up with somebody else for the night. (Except, perhaps, for the [unlucky?] wife who picked up her own husband's keys!)

Although almost everyone in the rec sex subculture has heard of the key party concept, no one seems to have actually done it or even know of anyone who has. Descriptions of this game may have been somewhat apocryphal and key parties may have been less of a reality and more of a creative fiction.

The content providers of that past era were eager to mine anything that seemed to reinforce the zeitgeist that a "sexual revolution" was taking place. These stories served a double purpose for the general public. The casual reader could cluck at the "immorality" of these people and, at the same time, get guilty pleasure in fantasizing about joining in their exploits.

The disappearance of the key party event (if it ever did occur much) is understandable in that it violated two of the most-commonly held values of the non-possessive subculture.

Firstly, in spite of what seems like a lot of sex-partner hopping, almost everyone in this lifestyle, and especially the women, want to make some conscious choice about who they will hook-up with. The randomness of the key party concept exposes participants to the risk of being stuck with a very undesirable sex partner and possibly for a lengthy period of time.

Secondly, in spite of possibly engaging in a lot of extra-relationship activity at a typical house party, almost all participating couples have an agreement to go home together as a way of reinforcing their bonding. As a variation on the "Save the last dance for me" theme, many couples have an agreement that, regardless of who they may each frolic with in the earlier part of the evening, they will have sex with each other as the last activity before leaving the party.

Spending the night and waking up in the morning with a new external sex partner is often out of bounds for most couples who are otherwise non-possessive. In spite of the liberal interpretation of their relationship commitments, factors such as this highlight the observation that there is actually a fair amount of relationship conservatism among these couples.

Contemporary non-possessive couples don't do key parties for these reasons. Historically, these events may have been a transitional phase between the earlier "wife-swapping" and the later swinging era as the broader culture moved away from the previous sexism toward more egalitarian values.

The key party phenomenon/ruse also illustrates the need to separate reality from the hyperbole generated by the popular media and a gullible audience hungry for scandalous revelations.

Meanwhile, across the pond, a distinctly European version of the house party concept has been playing out on the continent for centuries. In Germany, the Netherlands, and France, especially, there have long been secret "libertine" societies. Membership is generally limited to the very wealthy and powerful, with a sprinkling of celebrities.

These clandestine social networks often have as their primary function the organizing of elaborate soirees, involving the very best cuisine, wine, and, of course, sex. These "house parties" are frequently staged in the most elegant chateaux, often former castles and other similar mansions in secluded locations, with high security.

These are usually dress-up affairs with men in tuxedos and women in haute couture evening gowns. Alternatively, masks and the ceremonial robes of the society may be worn and the participants may engage in elaborate rituals, often adapted from pagan sexual practices.

Participation in these events is obviously a very guarded matter and those involved are extremely protective of their identity. Speculation has it, however, that these secret societies have members from the highest levels of business and government in Europe.

An Americanized version of the chateau sex scene is presented in the film *Eyes Wide Shut*,[9] wherein the uninvited Tom Cruise crashes the party with unfortunate results. When director Stanley Kubrick was asked if this film was made as a satire, with tongue in cheek, he allegedly replied that, actually, it was made with tongue in several cheeks.

Socials

"Conversation is the socializing instrument par excellence."[10]
—José Ortega y Gasset

Yet another variant on the rec sex continuum of events is the meet-and-greet type of gathering organized for the primary purpose of just encountering others with similar interests. No sex takes place at these "socials," which could be held at various public venues, such as the local dance hall or even the church recreation center!

Typically, at these socials, there is much mingling, conversation, drinking, and dancing but no overtly sexual activity. After some sizing up of erotic potential, those couples who wish to engage with each other go elsewhere (such as to the No-Tell Motel) to do so.

Frequently found in small towns and rural areas, these events are popular among the demographic at the other end of the socioeconomic scale from the Euro chateau set. Being rather low-budget affairs, socials are one of the most cost-effective ways for couples of modest means to explore non-possessive options.

Organizations with fixed locations that offer these events on a regular basis often use the term "off-premises club" to describe themselves and to differentiate what they provide from the (mainly) big-city, "on-premises" clubs which ordinarily have designated playrooms.

Enterprising couples can usually find online listings of such clubs in their local area along with membership information. Once signed up and vetted (no undercover vice-squad applicants, please), the couple is added to the e-mail contact list and can expect to receive invitations to upcoming events.

So, "Southside Socials" may send out a notice to its contact list of interested couples that there will be a cocktail party and dance next Saturday evening at the civic auditorium. If large enough, the organization may be able do a takeover of the entire place but, if not, may have to share the location with non-rec sex people.

To designate in-group members in this latter situation, creative symbols may be used such as specially-designated lapel pins or pendants. (Logos featuring bites out of apples are common.)

The in-group thus functions like a secret society within a general public setting, with members able to recognize each other, by reading the covert clues, but also able to conceal their status from outsiders.

Obviously, first encounters between couples who do not know each other proceed cautiously. One would not want to misinterpret that ambiguous piece of jewelry worn by the woman who later turns out to be the minister's wife.

Dogging

"Only mad dogs and Englishmen go out in the mid-day sun."[11]

—Noel Coward

Certain national cultures seem to have a propensity for developing innovative forms of non-possessive, intimate relationships. So it is with the British who have pioneered a quirky type of relating erotically, involving walking around among parked cars.

A couple in Britain who want to do some "dogging" will drive out to one of the well-known local sites (usually a secluded park area) and stop to wait for prospects. At the more popular times (for example, after the pubs close), there may be several dozen cars parked near to each other at these designated spots.

Several of the men will leave their cars to stroll around to approach those in the other cars. Single men will join in the foraging. Observing the passersby, some women in the cars may flash their headlights to indicate interest and/or availability.

A woman in a parked car may roll her window down to examine the visiting male more closely. Brief verbal interchanges may ensue. ("'Ello, luv, do ya fancy a little rumpy-pumpy?")

If the prospect is attractive enough, the woman may accommodate the bloke with some manual or oral stimulation, most often through the open window. Exceptionally attractive visitors may be invited inside (figuratively and literally) for a more full-service encounter.

Alternatively, the female may come out and lay on the bonnet (hood) or boot (trunk) of the car for a more al fresco experience. This option is obviously limited by the typically cold and wet weather in the United Kingdom. (Those thick British woolen blankets can sure come in handy on a chilly night.)

Eventually, the prowling male and the car-bound female of the couple who came together will reunite, perhaps compare notes regarding their respective adventures, and then drive home from the dogging site.

In addition to couples, there are usually a lot of optimistic solo men, often on foot, cruising through the parked car area looking for love (or at least lust) in all the right places. In fact, the term, "dogging" was apparently coined by such strollers who would tell the missus at home that they were just going out to walk the dog. (Such scoundrels!)

An alternate etymological theory, however, proposes that the term originated from the frequent practice of the female bending over the bonnet or the boot and doing it doggie-style. Whatever the word's origins, dogging is extremely popular in the United Kingdom, with many thousands of enthusiastic adherents.

With the current e-connectivity of almost everyone nowadays, dogging has expanded from the traditional, known locations to spontaneous gathering points and times. These can occur as sort of "flash mob" encounters for sex. (For example, #Dogging: tonight, 1:00 am, Queen's Park, Trafalgar statue)

Dogging appears to have developed in Great Britain as a do-it-yourself, no-cost alternative to rec sex clubs. As such, it offers a sort of au naturel playroom concept.

Capitalizing on the popularity of dogging, some British clubs have actually set up a car in one of their play areas! In these versions of indoor dogging, receptive females can sit in the car and service eager males pressing against the windows.

Dogging seems to be an almost entirely British phenomenon with little of this sort of activity occurring elsewhere in the world. (Leave it to the Brits to come up with yet another kinky sex practice.)

Perhaps imported from across the Channel, dogging has now become well-established in France, however. The scholarly reader who may be interested in (much) more exquisite detail is referred to *The Sexual Life of Catherine M.*[12] In this ostensibly accurate memoire, our intrepid heroine describes her extensive gang-bang sessions while dogging in the Bois de Boulogne of Paris. (Cherchez le chien!)

CHAPTER EIGHT

Threesomes, Foursomes, and Moresomes

Relationships are not limited to couples, of course. Any number of people can form a bonded unit in which the members share activities, values, and intimacy.

More specifically, three or more persons can enter into an agreement, whether explicit or tacit, in which they define themselves as an entity. As with couples, this agreement specifies how they will relate to each other and includes how these ways of relating to each other may be different from how they will relate to outsiders.

Consensual, non-possessive, intimate relationships are often observed among the several varieties of these multi-partner arrangements. In fact, for many, the open sharing of sexual partners is the primary reason for the formation of these more-than-two relationships.

This sharing may take place only among the members of the arrangement or may be extended to outsiders, depending on the rules of engagement agreed to by the members. Regardless of sexual sharing preferences, the three or more persons who comprise the multi-partner entity may be bonded in every other way as much as any monogamous couple.

Three's a Crowd?

"The chains of matrimony are so heavy, it takes three to bear them: myself, my wife, and my mistress."[1]

—Voltaire

In virtually all cultures, the sole acceptable format for intimate relationships is two persons only (preferably one male plus one female). All other combinations, meaning consensual intimate arrangements involving more than two persons, are universally considered temporary, unstable, and engaged in only by the morally challenged.

Three-way liaisons, whether fleeting or long-lasting, continue to occur, however. For heterosexuals, these can obviously be either of the Male/Female/Male or the Female/Male/Female variety. In either configuration, these combinations appear to offer the participants a way to explore and actualize non-possessive intimate arrangements within a relatively controlled framework.

Celebrities and creative artists often gain further notoriety by engaging in publicly revealed threesomes. (See *Henry and June*[2] for an entertaining biopic on one of the most famous three-ways, between the Millers and Anaïs Nin.)

Within the traditional world, almost without exception however, societal proscriptions against intimate triads require the reduction of these arrangements to a pair by elimination of one of the same-gender participants.

Sexual relationships involving three people are widely considered to be inevitably fraught with feelings of hostility and competitive behavior between the two persons of the same gender. Each is presumed to be motivated to banish the other from the relationship and to want to gain sole possession of the opposite-gender participant.

Hence, we see the "love triangle" as the single-most common theme in popular music, literature, film, and so on. The drama is provided by the conflict between the rivals to win the prize of the sexual favors and lasting affection of the third party. The plot resolution inevitably features the ejection of one of the same-gender participants from the relationship while the remaining two metaphorically ride off into the sunset together.

This scenario is embedded in virtually all cultural education and in the socialization process provided to young people almost everywhere and is repeated and reinforced incessantly in worldwide popular entertainment. With extremely few exceptions, it is not even imagined that there could be any other resolution to the love-triangle dilemma.

But what if instead of destroying the three-sided arrangement, the participants agreed to maintain it and become one bonded unit? What if they decided to become a trio rather than a couple plus one reject?

Historically, there appears to be scant reference to this type of resolution. Previous cultures grounded in conflict over possessions may have not been able to conceive of any other alternatives.

Besides, in our fictional archetypes, the dramatic possibilities are much more intense when people are attempting to destroy one another to possess a love object. Imagine how tame stories would be, from *Helen of Troy* through *Othello* to *Phantom of the Opera*, if everybody got along and just enjoyed each other!

Love-triangle conflicts are of antiquity. What is new is the significant, and apparently growing, number of people now experimenting with alternate forms of resolution of this age-old issue.

These adventuresome individuals are exploring how it would work to create a win-win-win outcome. Instead of rejecting one of the participants, they are rejecting the idea that the couple is the only stable form for an intimate relationship.

Three-way inclusive solutions offer several possible benefits to the participants:

- The same-gender members of the relationship may be able to reduce or even eliminate the conflict between themselves.
- Each of the same-gender members may be able to reduce or eliminate the anxiety regarding the possible loss of his/her shared love object.
- The opposite-gender member does not lose one of her/his partners and may continue to enjoy the benefits of having two lovers.
- All members benefit from the reduced stress of converting the relationship to a form that may be more stable.

For three persons to evolve into and maintain a successful, ongoing relationship among themselves, several adjustments are necessary:

- The two same-gender participants must be able to share the opposite-gender participant without significant feelings, or at least expressions, of jealousy, hostility, possessiveness, and so on.
- The same-gender participants must be able manage their anxieties regarding the possible loss of their shared love object and restructure their thinking to accept that exclusive control of her/him is not necessary.
- The same-gender participants must be able to transform their relationship with each other from one of competition to one of co-operation, or at least co-existence.
- The opposite-gender participant must be able to accept and share intimate attention from both of the same-gender participants without promoting, even covertly, any conflict between them.
- Relations with outsiders must be managed to avoid, or at least minimize, the effects of negative attitudes regarding three-way relationships on the part of significant others, such as family and friends.
- Logistical challenges must be managed for the trio to cope with a world that is almost exclusively couple-oriented (for example, beds are usually not large enough for three to sleep in comfortably).

For the same-gender participants, another obstacle, to sharing a sexual partner with someone of the same gender, is the possibility of same-sex contact and the feelings this may arouse. (This, of course, is much more of an issue for men than for women, who are generally a lot more tolerant of and even comfortable with, female-to-female affection.)

In either the M/F/M or the F/M/F configuration, for a triadic relationship to succeed, homophobic feelings need to be managed. Bisexuality is, of course, another option.

Relationship management becomes much more complex when more than two people are involved. Whereas, with a couple, there is only one relationship to focus on, in a triad, there are three relationships that must work well for the overall arrangement to succeed. Larry must get along with Curly, Curly must get along with Moe, and Moe must get along with Larry, for the threesome to remain together.

Many different types of arrangements are possible for structuring a three-sided relationship. At one end of the continuum, the three partners may all live together and share everything, including each other, without restrictions.

At the other extreme, there may be a "time-share" arrangement, in which each of the same-gender partners schedule their interaction with the opposite-gender partner and may rarely ever encounter each other. Several variants in between these two poles are possible also, of course.

The type and intensity of the relationships making up a threesome can vary greatly. Some are fully equilateral triangles, with both sexual and emotional intimacy shared by all three participants evenly. Another common model is the "V" pattern in which there is no bonding of any kind between the two same-gender participants, their only connection being the sharing of the opposite-gender member.

What defines the trio arrangement, and is common to all patterns, is the understanding and agreement that there are three stakeholders involved, each with certain rights and obligations. If either one of the same-gender participants is unaware of the other, this arrangement is clearly not fully consensual and deception must be involved.

In the deceptive case, which is extremely common in the possessive universe, the opposite-gender participant is "cheating," either singly or doubly, and the three-way relationship is neither mutually agreed to nor likely to be stable.

In spite of the enormous range of diversity found in the topics considered by the arts, when it comes to relationship models, it is almost impossible to find positive examples of anything other than the standard one-plus-one arrangement. It seems curious that so few of our authors, playwrights, songwriters, and other creative types have even considered that there could be stable and mutually-satisfying intimate relationships involving more than two persons. ("What if, for example, Rick got on that last flight to Lisbon along with Ilsa and Victor[3] and they all went off to share a new life together?")

Ménage Management

"A love triangle is just a threesome delayed."[4]

—Mokokoma Mokhonoana

Just as with couples who have stable non-possessive relationships, successful triadic arrangements appear to be based on honest communication, mutual trust, and harm avoidance.

Because there are three times the number of relationships in a threesome, as compared to a couple, there are potentially three times the number of ways the arrangement can fall apart. Any significant conflict between any two of the partners can potentially scuttle the entire three-way partnership.

The good news is that there is an additional person to help with conflict resolution. In a couple, when the two partners are antagonistic to each other, no one else is intimately involved. If help is needed, the couple must turn to outside parties who may not be knowledgeable enough or caring enough to assist with resolution.

In a triadic relationship, when two of the partners are experiencing conflict, the third can often assist as a knowledgeable and unbiased arbitrator and may be able to facilitate rapprochement between the quarreling partners.

For those who haven't done it yet, engaging in a three-way encounter is an extremely prevalent focus of wishful thinking. (A Google search of "threesomes" will turn up over a million sites.) Getting it on with two women simultaneously is obviously a big-time male fantasy, as any scan of the porn titles featuring this combo will reveal.

Most women are "tri-curious" also and wonder what it would be like to be pleasured by two men concurrently. After they lose their "tri-virginity" both men and women may find themselves becoming "tri-sexual," strongly preferring the triadic over the dyadic form of frolicking. If they bond together and exclude outsiders, the threesome could be considered, "trinogamous."

Threesomes rarely occur because three unattached people spontaneously decide to get together. Almost always, there is an existing relationship between two persons and these two decide to bring a third person into their partnership.

Most commonly, an opposite-gender couple may agree to add someone else to share intimacies with. Less commonly, but still occurring with some frequency, two same-gender friends may conspire to form a threesome with an opposite-gender partner.

To form a temporary threesome, male/female couples appear to choose an extra partner for the goose or one for the gander with about equal frequency. This situation offers multiple possibilities for the politics of sexual negotiation, with some couples reporting strategies such as, "This time for you, next time for me."

When threesomes are formed at the initiation of two same-gender friends, it is most often two men who recruit a female to share. Female friends are generally less likely to initiate conjoint acquisition and sharing of a new male partner (other than at bachelorette parties).

Because almost all threesomes are formed via a two-plus-one process, opportunities exist here for single individuals to engage in relationships with existing partners. In comparison to swinging, which is heavily singles-averse, the unattached tend to find a more welcoming experience within the context of the threesome scene.

For singles interested in engaging with existing couples, this type of arrangement may offer several types of benefits. Individuals seeking physical intimacy only, men for example, can find satisfaction without the "risk" of unwanted emotional demands since the opposite-gender partner already has a (presumably) committed relationship. Bisexual opportunities, especially for women, are another benefit for singles engaging with couples.

Some singles are looking for a more bonded relationship and may perceive an established couple as offering more security than other unattached singles. The appeal for these singles is that of finding a couple who can take care of both their sexual and their emotional needs.

Although many of these three-way liaisons are transitory, some evolve into more permanent triads, in which the former single is accorded more or less equal status with the partners of the original couple.

Among the general public, socialization/cultural pressures to adapt to the standard couples-only model are so strong and discussions of alternatives so non-existent that almost no one even thinks that anything else may be possible. The traditional perspective is that any ménage-à-trois is a perversion, or at best, a temporary and unstable aberration.

In mainstream culture, any bonding among three people that involves sexual activity is almost never considered to be a possible basis for a long-term and mutually-supportive relationship. The universal dualistic relationship model is founded on the assumption that a person cannot love, or at least cannot truly love, more than one person at the same time.

And yet, many long-term, three-way relationships belie this assumption. The partners in many of these bonded threesomes are clearly in love with each other in the deepest way and the love of each partner for the other two is not diminished by the fact that it is shared.

When it comes to intimate relationships, the entertainment arts of popular culture relentlessly reinforce the three's-a-crowd concept. One rare exception is found in the 1967 pop song "Triad,"[5] written by David Crosby, in which Grace Slick asks, "Why can't we go on as three?" (My thanks to Tom Robbins for identifying this singular instance of a creative resolution to the triangulation problem.)

Playing Mixed Doubles

"Tennis, anyone?"[6]

—Humphrey Bogart

Trio relationships may be expanded by adding yet another participant. The new partner could be of the same gender as the two same-sex members, creating a 3 + 1 arrangement. Although some of these configurations appear to do well, they are often dogged by logistical complications and possible physiological limits (especially if everyone is hetero and the sole-gender participant is male).

More balanced are 2M + 2F configurations, which are the most common form of four-way arrangements. Again, multiple types of sexual and emotional relationships may develop between and among the participants of these foursomes. As was so titillatingly expressed in the subtitle to *Bob & Carol & Ted & Alice*,[7] "Consider the possibilities."

As with trios, the intensity of the involvements can vary greatly. At one end of the range, some foursomes may get together only periodically and just for swapped sex, akin to the swingers' model. At the other commitment pole, the four may live together and share all resources including each other, without restriction. In the most extreme form of these 2×2 relationships, no two participants may be more bonded than any other two.

Two-by-two arrangements can be exclusively hetero or not, depending on the level of interest/comfort with bisexual activities. Frolicking may be limited to one-on-one encounters, which may take place behind closed doors or openly, or may include multiple-partner sessions.

Foursomes have the advantage of being easier than threesomes to mask from social disapproval. Two couples sharing a large house, for example, may be able to present themselves as two monogamous relationships, just sharing living space together for economic reasons.

In the most common foursome format, however, two couples each live separately but define themselves as a single bonded unit. They have a consensual, non-possessive intimate relationship in that each member of each couple has sex with the opposite-gender member of the other couple, with everyone's knowledge and approval.

Many of these long-term, four-way units may be considered exclusivist, in that they do not engage in sexual activities with outsiders. They may be "fluid bonded" in that, because there are no external intimacies, there is no need for condoms or other safe-sex practices.

These committed quadripartite relationships function much like those of traditional married couples. There are just more spouses involved in the union.

Each "husband" may think of himself as having two "wives" and each "wife" may see herself as having two "husbands." (Scheduling anniversary celebrations can become quite complex.)

Group Gropes

"The more, the merrier."[8]

—John Heywood

Any number of people may enter into an arrangement to have intimate relationships with each other on some more or less frequent basis. These consensual groups may take many forms but two varieties seem to be the most common.

In one version, a cluster of people, each living independently or as couples, get together periodically for erotic sessions hooking up with each other in either 1:1 or larger configurations. At times, these sessions are pre-planned and happen on a regular basis (for example, every Saturday night at Charlie Sheen's place).

With the recent explosive growth of sexting, however, sessions can be spontaneously convened by the group, much in the manner of flash mobs. What often defines these flesh(?) mobs as relationship-based is that members of the group are generally all aware of each other and each usually participates sexually with each opposite-gender other, although frequencies may vary depending on level of interest, availability, and so on.

Although there have been some reports of attempts at crowdsourcing for creating a larger erotic encounter, these efforts typically succeed in producing only a batch of hopeful men. (Probably best not to try this with all of your Facebook friends.)

In the second version, which we might call the "commune" model, a small number of people may live together and share each other sexually along with sharing household expenses, residential maintenance duties, etc.

This non-possessive group option has evolved as a more modern iteration of the "group marriage" concept practiced by several early religious organizations (which was sort of an example of sex among the sects). Although peaking in popularity in the neo-hippie era of the 1970s, these arrangements appear to be much less frequent now.

One of the best-known of these "intentional communities" was the Kerista Commune,[9] which flourished in the 1970s and 1980s in San Francisco. Keristans took a vow of "polyintimacy" in which they pledged to have sex only with others (and all others) who were members.

Of all of the weird and wonderful aspects of the Kerista quasi-religion, none attracted more media attention than the (scandalous!) "sleeping schedule." Each month, a new list was posted showing, for each night, who was to sleep with whom and in what bedroom. By pairing up each member with each opposite-gender member, this full rotation through the roster certainly ensured nightly variety.

The Kerista tribe pioneered STI testing as a requirement for group membership (probably a good idea for that location at that time) and required all males to have a vasectomy(!) as a method of birth control. By the 1990s, however, the Kerista Commune faded away (possibly because of the lack of offspring to carry it onwards).

Intimate-relationship groups vary greatly in terms of their openness to outsiders. Policies and procedures may range from admitting any willing participant to lengthy screening and testing requirements for new applicants.

The most restrictive groups are often "fluid bonded," foregoing STI protection and agreeing to have sex only with other members of the group. So, although they are non-possessive within their group, they could be considered to be possessive, vis-à-vis outsiders.

In a sense then, these closed groupings function somewhat like a traditional, monogamous relationship, only with multiple husbands and multiple wives.

Polygamous "marriages" may also qualify as group-based intimate relationships but must be considered as only quasi non-possessive because there is usually a strict double standard of exclusiveness. Typically, the multiple-gender participants agree to share the sole gender participant but the sole gender participant generally demands exclusive control over the intimate activities of the multiple-gender participants.

These harem-like arrangements are almost all polygynous (literally, "many vaginas") and are invariably composed of one male with several females. The polyandrous versions occur so infrequently as to be sources of fascination for cultural anthropologists.

In these unions, the female participants may all have equal status. Alternatively, one may be the official "wife" with the others adopting the role of concubines. (See *Raise the Red Lantern*[10] for an entertaining presentation of the Chinese version of this type of quasi non-possessive intimate relationship.)

Some quasi-commercial versions of multi-partner arrangements can also be found. A specific instance (which I observed and in which I interviewed some of the participants) illustrates one variation. In this set-up, a young man, whom we'll call "Randy," came into some inheritance money and used it to buy a small rooming house near a college campus.

Randy rented out each of the six rooms to students but chose only attractive young women to be his tenants. He then negotiated a rent-exemption agreement with each of them such that, on Monday night he stopped by Karen's room to collect the "rent" from her, on Tuesday night he visited Joyce to collect her rent, and so on. (And, on the seventh night, he rested, presumably.)

One interesting thing about this somewhat patriarchal arrangement was how well it seemed to work for all parties. The women seemed quite happy to have free accommodation in return for a relatively minimal inconvenience (one date night a week taken up). Randy, however, always seemed to look exhausted.

Nobody put any restrictions on anybody and the women involved were all sexually active with other boyfriends on other nights. Any woman was free to exit the Landlord-Tenant Agreement at any time but, when this occurred, there never seemed to be any lack of willing replacements.

Another interesting phenomenon was the somewhat unexpected bonding among the tenants. The women in the house would get together frequently as a group and, over the course of some tequila, would have great fun sharing stories about Randy's peculiarities in bed.

In each of these examples of group-based non-possessive intimate relationships, membership can be somewhat fluid with, at times, some participants leaving and new recruits being brought in. Often, existing members must approve new candidates for admission. Some cult-like groups may also have formalized sexual initiation rituals in which potential new admissions are evaluated for suitability.

Inner-city gangs may make membership offers to select females contingent upon such initiation rituals, for example. In one common version, the female applicant is required to have sex sequentially with several or all of the gang members. See Anne Hathaway in *Havoc*[11] for a dramatization of this practice commonly known in the gangsta community as "pulling a train."

Orgy Options

"What are you doing after the orgy?"

—Woody Allen[12]

Those promoting intimate group activities generally advance the proposition that if adding one or two more to a couple increases the pleasure opportunities, why not add several more?

As with threesomes and foursomes, however, addition may lead to multiplication, especially of potential problems. Basic matters to be negotiated and resolved may include gender balance (1 to 1 or some other ratio?) and orientation style (only hetero, bi OK for females, or free-style wrestling with no holds barred?).

Those who participate in group-based sex activities may have their choice of sequential or simultaneous interactions. In the former, a participant may limit their contact to one partner at a time but rotate through several that may be available. In the latter, the participant may invite several of those who are willing to pleasure her or him concurrently. (Although this is a big-time male fantasy, it is most often the women who are successful in recruiting multiple volunteers.)

Couples, especially the less experienced, often see participation in group sex activities as kind of a black-belt level of non-possessiveness. Both performance skills and emotional control may be tested as a participant tries to concentrate on their current playmate while watching their honey getting it on repeatedly with any willing sex object.

When the general public hears talk of groups having intimate relationships among their members, they often imagine orgy scenes from porn movies. Hyped by the media and perhaps fantasized by the inhibited, orgies are visualized as a puppy pile of people all pleasuring one another indiscriminately. A sort of an extreme *Girls (and Boys) Gone Wild* episode, the orgy is seen as the ultimate in degenerate behavior by those with more Puritan values.

The reality is that full-on, unrestricted group orgies are not all that prevalent. Selection factors still rule, even among the most uninhibited. Preferences prevail and even in group settings, people still choose who to engage with and how much. Many rec sex clubs have one or more so-called "orgy rooms," for example, but in these it is unusual to find anything more than individual couples pairing up.

Historically, ongoing consensual intimate groupings have had the briefest lifespans of all types of alternative relationships. It seems to take a rare combination of individuals who are able to create and maintain a successful and lasting group arrangement involving sexual and/or emotional bonding among multiple members.

Transient group encounters have a certain appeal among those who want to share intimacy with several others, however. Many rec sex clubs and events, for example, organize erotic multi-partner warm-up activities that may or may not lead to full-body contact sports.

Perhaps following the well-known adage that "many hands make light work," one of the most popular of these preliminaries is the group massage session. In this activity, three or four couples may gather around a massage table and each person takes a turn being rubbed all over by everybody else simultaneously. Often, the recipient may specify how intimate a massage is preferred, using appropriateness categories like those used for films, such as PG, R, or X-rated.

Ice-breaking warm-ups, often adapted from Tantra exercises, are sometimes taught in group workshops. These "pujas" may involve, for example, two concentric circles of participants, one male and one female.

When the music starts, each person may have two minutes to provide, as directed by the workshop leader, some kind of stimulation to the person directly across from them. When the music stops, one circle rotates one position to pair up new partners and the activity resumes. (Most participants claim that the children's game of "musical chairs" was never this much fun.)

CHAPTER NINE

Polyamory

The word "polyamory" is itself a cohabitation of Greek and Latin meanings and is generally understood to be translated as "many loves." More specifically, polyamory is usually defined as the practice of having more than one loving relationship simultaneously, with the consent of everyone involved.

Although polyamorous relationships have probably existed since the dawn of time, the word itself was only coined as a neologism in the early 1990s.[1] The term gained widespread acceptance as a way to describe the many forms of multi-partner arrangements that had evolved in the previous free-thinking decades.

As a type of non-possessive intimate relationship, polyamory is a more all-inclusive term than polygamy (in either its polygynous or polyandrous forms), which generally is taken to mean having more than one spouse.

Polyamorous relationships do not require a wedding ceremony. In fact, marriage among more than two individuals is not legally allowed in any Western country. Although some polyamorous units may consider themselves to be in a group marriage, to actually implement this would potentially expose them to anti-bigamy sanctions.

Loving More

"I reserve the right to love many people at once."[2]

—Anaïs Nin

The sine qua non of poly relationships is the emphasis on full disclosure, negotiation, and acceptance by all parties of the multi-partner arrangement.

Poly people have high regard for the values of honesty, transparency, openness, and respect for others in the partnership. Defining polyamory as ethical non-monogamy, polyamorists see themselves as a morally superior alternative to undisclosed non-monogamy, that is, "cheating."

Polyamory can be distinguished from recreational sex in several ways. Most simply, those in the rec sex lifestyle emphasize the erotic aspects of their multiple interactions while polyamorists focus more on the romantic and emotional bonding elements of their relationships.

Swinging encounters, for example, are frequently brief and transient. Polyamory arrangements usually take time to develop and often endure for years. Sex among those in "the lifestyle" is generally regarded as play or recreation whereas among polyamorists, sex is most often seen as a way to solidify and deepen personal attachments.

As alternative forms of non-possessiveness, however, swinging and polyamory have much in common. Both reject the standard viewpoint that sexual exclusiveness is necessary for a lasting and committed relationship. Among poly as well as swing adherents, the values of honesty, transparency, and consensual agreements are paramount. Each style attracts both men and women who have a strong need for sexual variety.

The majority of poly arrangements seem to be made up of three partners, either FMF or MFM. As such, they function much like the triads discussed in the previous chapter describing threesomes.

While many casual three-way arrangements are quite fluid, poly triforms are generally much more stable, however. These are most often created by an existing couple adding a single person as a more or less permanent partner in their relationship.

As with all relationships, and especially non-possessive arrangements, agreements form an essential part of the polyamorous union. Rules, boundaries, schedules, and so on are typically negotiated among all partners and expectations are formalized, often more explicitly than in other non-poly relationships.

The need for a more structured agreement is often simply due to the larger number of people involved but is also influenced by the fact that there are not just sexual issues to consider but emotional/romantic ones as well.

Complexities in poly arrangements can be illustrated by considering just the multiple erotic possibilities inherent in the simplest, three-partner form. In the most complete version of this poly level, each person in the triad would have sex with each other person, including the same gender combination, and all three would have sex together as a threesome. In less complete versions, such as the "V" configuration, only one person would have sex with each of the other two and they, typically the same-gender members, would not have sex with each other.

In poly arrangements, love relationships need to be considered also. Again, in a poly threesome, all three partners may love one another equally or there may not be a love attachment between any two of the persons involved.

Poly unions involving more than three persons, expand the possibilities exponentially. An outside observer might understandably be confused by these multi-partner unions when being told who is in love with whom and who is having sex with whom. To avoid the dreaded Abbott and Costello "Who's on First?"[3] routine, a visual representation of the players and the interrelationships is helpful.

A sociogram, such as the one in the illustration, is a way to represent the pattern of multi-partner connections in a specific multi-partner union. Because relationships and even the persons involved tend to be fluid, especially in larger clusters, it may be best to draw such diagrams in pencil.

Polyfidelity

"Unus pro omnibus, omnes pro uno."[4]

—d'Artagnan

In addition to relations with others within the poly unit, the partners in the arrangement need to consider interactions with outsiders as well. Some poly people are relatively open to sexual and romantic encounters with out-group persons and even to recruiting others to join as partners. Other poly unions are closed to outsiders and the partners agree to forego intimate relations of any kind with outsiders.

The term "polyfidelity" has been suggested to describe this latter form of agreement. Although such closed poly groupings would not be considered monogamous by anyone's definition, nevertheless, they function much like a traditional exclusivist couple, the only difference being that there are more than two "spouses."

Adding to the complexity of the various types of poly arrangements, the common occurrence of hierarchies must be considered. Some partners may be more equal than others. For example, a married couple that brings a third person into their intimacy, may consider their relationship to this person as secondary while their marriage remains the primary bond. Generally, secondary relationships involve fewer rights and responsibilities as compared to primary relationships.

Like just almost everyone, people who gravitate toward polyamory are looking for love. (If sex comes along with the love, that's a bonus.) The big difference from the mainstream culture is that poly people reject the notion that love needs to be limited to only one other person at a time. Those of the polyamorous persuasion believe that deeply committed loving relationships can be formed and maintained among more than two people simultaneously.

With numerous websites, conferences, books, articles, and blogs (look for titles such as "Loving More," "Love Unlimited," "Love in Abundance,"[5] and so on), polyamory is a burgeoning subculture. Aside from a few sensationalist media reports, it flies below the radar of the general population.

There appear to be (mostly covert) poly units in virtually every community, however, and these multi-lovers face the same issues of dealing with disapprobation from the traditional "family" values majority as do those engaging in all other forms of non-possessive relationships.

As contrasted to a sexual orientation, such as the familiar GLBT spectrum, polyamory may be considered a relationship orientation. Some polyamorists feel that multiple, simultaneous loving is the natural human way and that this perhaps originally pagan relationship style was corrupted by the rise of organized religions that used monogamy as a method to control sexual impulses.

Other than a few Poly Pride displays, however, there have been relatively few attempts at political activism or to gain more acceptance or rights for the poly oppressed.

Poly people are big on symbols. The infinity sign superimposed onto a heart is a common representation used to identify adherents. Flags and ribbons with blue, red, and black representing openness, passion, and solidarity are frequently seen at poly gatherings.

The blue, red, and black parrot has achieved some currency as yet another symbol of polyamory. (Polly want a what?) Some unintended irony may be perceived in this choice of mascot because ornithologists consider parrots to be among the most monogamous of birds.

As with other non-possessive relationship styles, the acceptance of polyamory generally requires some psychological adjustments. In traditional Western culture, almost everyone grows up being socialized to believe that intimate relationships can only be binary and exclusivist. To accept that sex and even love can be shared with multiple others concurrently and consensually is a major epiphany.

To get there, potential poly practitioners usually need to overcome various types of cognitive and emotional resistance. These are often expressed in terms of freeing oneself from feelings of possessiveness, jealousy, the need to have control of others, etc.

A typical married couple, for example, may have some interest in transitioning their relationship to be less exclusive in some way and may be exploring various non-possessive alternatives. If they consider swinging as an option, each of them will need to be comfortable with their spouse having sex with other people.

To consider polyamory, however, is to contemplate a whole other level. Not only would the husband and the wife need to be OK with their spouse having sex with others but also comfortable with that spouse potentially developing a deeply committed love relationship with another person.

Allowing, supporting, and even encouraging the one you love to seek and develop loving relationships with others can be seen as a very threatening concept to most traditionalists. To poly practitioners, however, loving others is not a threat but is in fact the purpose of human interaction.

Most polyamorists believe that love should be shared with as many people as possible and not limited to only one person at a time. They may advise people to calmly accept that it is human nature to have multiple loving relationships simultaneously and that this is a good thing.

As such, poly people are somewhat unique within the spectrum of different types of non-possessive relationships, in their emphasis on love rather than sex as the basis for shared intimacy. They might tweak the title of this book to be *Relax, It's Just Love*.

CHAPTER TEN

Friends with Benefits

In addition to married couples and people involved in bonded multi-partner arrangements, individuals who define themselves as single also form consensual non-possessive intimate relationships. The previously ubiquitous serial monogamy style of dating that used to be described by terms such as "going steady" or "seeing someone" has been steadily declining in popularity, however, and is being replaced by a more fluid form of social/sexual networking.

As with non-possessive couples and groups, single people who develop non-traditional relationships with others often incorporate into these arrangements some form of recreational sex. The term "rec sex" implies, here also, that the erotic activity is engaged in primarily because it is regarded as enjoyable as an end in and of itself and is not necessarily intended to be a means of accomplishing some other goal, such as mate acquisition or procreation.

Even more radically, sex for recreational purposes need not fulfill any other commonly accepted monogamy-based function, such as creating or maintaining emotional bonding between the sexual partners.

As with so many other aspects of contemporary life, the exponential growth and constant evolution of electronic communication technologies have offered dramatically enhanced possibilities for new forms of social interaction and especially for those involving sex among singles.

Booty Calls

"Why don't you come up and see me sometime?"[1]

—Mae West

A recently well-publicized phenomenon, which nicely illustrates the non-possessive mindset, is the burgeoning social networks of people who initiate communication with each other for the explicit purpose of having ASAP sex. A booty call occurs when one person contacts another person, by voice/text/e-mail/etc., to propose an erotic encounter in the very near future.

Typically, booty calls are made between people who already know each other (and almost always have had sex with each other previously) and are rarely used as an attempt at first-time seduction. Booty calls may be distinguished also from the usual date soliciting in which the proposal is for a more traditional activity, such as dinner, a movie, and so on, at least initially.

Booty calls can be distinguished also from date invitations in that booty calls are often made at times outside those customary for dating, such as late at night or in the early-morning hours. Whereas traditional date proposals usually project some future time for the get-together, booty calls most often convey a sense of urgency, requesting a liaison now!

Men, of course, are most often the callers but, increasingly, women are taking the initiative to booty call, although they may still feel the need to be more subtle regarding their intentions. ("Tyrone, I know it's late but I'm having trouble sleeping and I was hoping you would be able to come over and bring some hot chocolate to help me relax.")

Regardless of gender, the receiver of a booty call may accept or reject the invitation based on factors such as the receiver's mood, interest in the caller, other options available, and so on. For those in the booty-calling sub-culture, the making and receiving of these invitations is generally treated in a very matter-of-fact manner, much as a suggestion to go have coffee would be. Rarely is there any ill will or stigma attached to getting or giving a rejection to a booty call.

The person demurring may just suggest that the caller try again another time when circumstances may be more favorable. The caller may simply try another candidate for the present time.

The social dynamics inherent in booty calling are noteworthy in that this phenomenon did not exist, at least in a widespread way, a couple of decades ago. The rapid evolution and acceptance of instant-messaging technologies has allowed this relatively new form of sexual communication to proliferate to a point where there are well-established booty-calling social networks just about everywhere now.

Those involved in these booty-calling networks still represent a relatively small percentage of the general population but their numbers and their visibility in the popular media have increased dramatically since the 1990s. Booty callers and responders tend to be young, urban, attractive, and sophisticated people of both genders. For them, booty calling provides a short-term way of meeting a need when more traditional options are not as readily available.

As is so often the case with new sexual phenomena, the gay subculture pioneered the model for booty calling long before the hetero world caught on to its benefits. Many single gays have one or more "butt buddies" whom they can contact for the prospect of sexual gratification on short notice.

Among straights, there are, in some big-city locations, relatively large and loosely interconnected networks of people consensually involved in this type of hook-up arrangement. A well-connected "metrosexual" (of either gender) may have a dozen or more names on their calling "rotation" and when the need arises, they simply go down the list until a positive response is obtained. Similarly, an exceptionally desirable recipient may receive several booty-call invitations in one evening.

The emergence of the booty-call phenomenon illustrates how contemporary sexual relationships often emphasize practical rather than idealistic values. The booty-call arrangement is a very functional method of obtaining sexual satisfaction without the perceived excess baggage of dating, romance, commitment, etc.

Not that those involved in booty calling necessarily disdain romance and love relationships. Booty calling simply offers, to both men and women, an immediate solution to a sexual need situation when more traditional alternatives are not currently viable.

Among those who have a booty-calling relationship, sexual fidelity is obviously not part of the arrangement. Those making and responding to booty calls are clearly non-monogamous. Anyone attempting to enforce any possessiveness of anyone else would be voted off the island of that network.

To some extent, booty callers/responders have chosen to replace the traditional one-partner-only form of relationship with an arrangement which provides them with multiple sexual partners on an on-demand basis. Booty calling arrangements may perhaps be viewed as extreme versions of serial monogamy in which the exclusiveness only lasts for one night at a time, or less.

A frequently mentioned benefit is the sense of being connected to a network of like-minded people with whom callers and recipients have relatively frequent communication and interaction, both intimate and otherwise. The sense of being desired and accepted by others in the calling interchange is another commonly perceived benefit.

Booty-Calling Perks

Carly Rae Jepsen got everybody lip-synching in 2012 with her catchy pop tune "Call Me Maybe."[2] Her lyrics captured the common practice among young girls of disclosing digits and requesting a response.

Perhaps somewhat surprising to outsiders, booty-calling relationships are often based on much more than just sex. Many of these relationships involve single people, without other long-term bonded partners, who provide closeness and emotional support to each other as well as an erotic connection. In this sense, the sexual benefits are a sort of an icing on the friendship cake.

In another variation, some married or otherwise bonded couples may use booty calling as a way to enhance sexual stimulation in their relationship. In one form of these arrangements, one or both partners may be granted booty-calling "privileges" to and from outsiders.

Similar to other types of non-possessive unions, these agreements attempt to combine the best of alternative lifestyles. When these arrangements work well, they allow the partners of the couple to balance relationship stability with external sexual variety.

A couple may also develop a booty-call arrangement within their own relationship! In this type of agreement, the understanding is that either of the partners may contact the other to request (or demand) a sexual encounter on short notice. To maintain discretion, some couples may develop coded messages for this purpose. (Animal mating calls seem to be popular.)

In addition to in-house booty calls by couples currently being intimate, these arrangements can be found with some frequency between the partners of a previously bonded couple who are no longer together. Perhaps surprisingly, such arrangements do occur, at times, between men and women who are no longer married to each other. In this context, they may be called ex-sex booty calls.

These ex-sex arrangements thus represent a pragmatic compromise resolution of a relationship in which, although many other aspects of the pairing may have been unsatisfactory, the sex was still great. The formerly bonded partners thus, very pragmatically, keep the best part of the relationship and abandon the rest.

When these "between the sheets" arrangements work well, they provide, for both the male and the female, a relatively secure option for meeting physical intimacy needs without any other extraneous expectations.

As with all social/sexual interactions, gender differences play a role in booty calling. For men, having a booty-call relationship with one or more women has obvious advantages. When the need for sex arises, a simple communication may provide a satisfying resolution for the man.

Being able to access non-commercial sex while not having to engage in some form of the mating dance has great appeal for most men. The revelation that this can occur is sort of like, "Oh, there's an app for that too?"

The content of incoming and outgoing booty calls is often shared with close friends. A man who can send a message and shortly thereafter be in bed with the recipient gains much respect from his peers, both male and female. His status is further enhanced when he is the recipient. ("Sorry, guys, I gotta go; it's another booty call.")

For women who participate in booty call arrangements, some of the same advantages apply but with different dynamics. Whereas men may consummate a booty call ASAP with any available female on their calling list, women are generally much more selective as to with who and when.

Even if a woman rejects a booty call invitation, being invited still provides some confirmation that she is attractive, sexually desirable, etc. On the other side of the arrangement, being free to contact a man with the explicit purpose of proposing sex is, for some women, the ultimate expression of female empowerment and gender equality.

Being involved in one or more booty call relationships may be especially appealing to women with strong sexual needs. The prospect of having, perhaps in a single evening, several invitations to choose from can be very stimulating to the sexually active female.

For the woman who insists on having only high-quality male performance, the booty call arrangement allows her to get her needs met with men she knows will be up to her expectations (literally). Some women, for example, update their list of callers with something like a multi-star system, based on the caller's past effectiveness in providing sexual satisfaction. (See *Bridget Jones's Diary.*[3])

For many women, using a booty calling network involving familiar callers is far preferable to the alternatives, such as trolling with girlfriends or waiting alone in pick-up bars, which may lead to potentially risky encounters with strangers and/or the unskilled. (See *Looking for Mr. Goodbar.*[4]) Accepting a booty call from a friend with benefits and known qualities is seen as a much safer and more conservative option.

For both men and women, booty calling offers several advantages in terms of simplifying aspects of relationships which can otherwise get quite complex. Booty calling arrangements are often valued for their directness and honesty. Although it may be thinly veiled to be a bit more socially acceptable ("Would you like to join me at my place tonight for a drink?") the intent of the message is generally quite obvious.

Among those involved in the non-possessive, booty-calling subculture, the making and receiving of sexual invitation calls is treated as a routine part of everyday life. Both callers and recipients are aware that the activity is consensual and playful. By contrast, in mainstream society, contacting someone with the express purpose of proposing a sexual encounter would be considered, at the very least, in poor taste and could even result in sexual harassment allegations.

In the booty call social networks, however, recipients generally appreciate the request, even if they don't accept it this time. For those mostly young, attractive, urban sophisticates who have these arrangements, the booty call is seen as an elegant solution to the age-old problem for both genders, namely, how to get good sex when you need it.

Among those who participate, there is generally little or no anguish or embarrassment over being rejected or rejecting a booty call invitation. Rejection typically involves a "Not tonight but try me another time" expression. As such, these communications generally display a mutual respect between the parties involved.

Although the request is for "casual" sex with no other strings attached, in fact, in these relationships, there are most often at least some emotionally-bonding elements. Frequently, booty calling evolves between or among people who have been or still are lovers, friends, neighbors, and so on.

Previously established feelings of mutual support, trust, caring, and affection often continue to guide the relationship as it morphs into a booty-call arrangement. Again, this type of sexual hook-up can be contrasted with those that generally lack these attributes, such as one-night stands with strangers.

As in so many other areas, the rapid evolution of communication technologies is continuing to transform how we engage in intimate relationships. Nowadays, booty calls are most often transmitted in text format. Text-based communications allow for some refinements in wording for both caller and respondent.

For the caller, a message can be crafted and edited to present a more favorably expressed invitation than might be possible in spontaneous speaking. For the person being called, the receipt of a booty-call text offers time to reflect, consider, and compose a more thoughtful response than might be the case with the voice-to-voice alternative.

A "how-to" manual could probably be written on the fine art of sending and responding to booty calls. Messages are rarely as blatant as, "Hey Juliet, this is Romeo. Would you like to have sex with me tonight?" Somewhere, someone is probably compiling a list of the booty-call phrases most likely to succeed.

CHAPTER ELEVEN

The Appeal of Non-Possessive Intimate Relationships

People are attracted to non-traditional forms of relationships for many reasons. Disillusionment with the standard model and its inherent restrictions may prompt couples and singles to explore alternatives. For those involved in possessive arrangements, the passage of time may exacerbate the dissatisfactions and frustrations of strict monogamy. (See *The Seven-Year Itch*.[1])

Several studies have indeed confirmed that divorce rates peak at around seven years. This observation has prompted a few suggestions that there should be "term limits" on marriages. One European proposal would require all marriage licenses (like most other licenses) to have an expiration date. In this plan, the couple would need to apply for a renewal, if they wanted to continue, or if not, their union would be automatically dissolved after seven years.[2]

Not waiting for government action on this issue, non-possessive couples have evolved their own plans for a kind of sabbatical to meet their needs for continued relationship intimacy.

Most of these non-possessives are looking to build some of the benefits of being single into their married lifestyle. The partners in these unions often have a higher than average need for satisfying sexual stimulation and are attracted to the excitement of unconventional activities.

Many of these people reject exclusivity as an ethical matter, seeking to eschew the evils of jealous control and aggression. In addition to meeting these moral imperatives, couples frequently find that the non-possessive alternative helps them cope with common life changes, such as with ageing and loss.

Adopting a non-possessive style for their relationship is appealing to those couples who desire to live and love in a way often extolled by poets and free thinkers as the highest human purpose. In this way, they meet their needs to not limit the freedom of those they love or themselves.

Those who see the non-possessive forms of intimate relationships as attractive are usually attempting to hedge against the widely-perceived-as-inevitable decline of intensity, passion, and possibly commitment. They are essentially asking the question, "Can we keep love alive by not making it so restrictive?"

Expanding Awareness

"True love in this differs from gold and clay,
That to divide is not to take away."[3]

—Percy Bysshe Shelley

For most traditional couples, the idea of trying a non-possessive form of their relationship, if it's thought about at all, is quickly dismissed as unrealistic. ("Nobody does that.") Some people, however, seem to be motivated by a need to look beyond the usual societal proscriptions and seek innovative solutions to relationship problems.

Those couples that actually explore how a non-exclusive arrangement might work often start by thinking through how relationships function and may come to the realization that, "Wait a minute, maybe there's something in this non-possessive thing that would work for us." Their analysis may include some or all of the following concepts.

A relationship may be said to exist when there is an agreement between two (or more) people that each person commits to (either explicitly or tacitly) and that provides guidance/restrictions as to what the relationship partners may or may not do and that is expected to persist over time (although the terms of the agreement may change).

An intimate relationship includes the additional elements of emotional attachment and/or sexual interaction between the partners. Non-possessive intimate relationships include a still further component in that, in these arrangements, the partners do not attempt to exert control over, or ownership of, at least some aspects of each other's intimate behavior.

Although the partners in these non-possessive intimate relationships may agree that each is free to engage in some sexual and/or romantic interactions with others, these liberties are generally not absolute. Most commonly, the partners have some understanding as to the limits on the freedoms given to each other.

Possessive intimate relationships are the standard in virtually all cultures, across all time periods and even in much of the animal kingdom. Possessive intimate relationships usually include elements such as the following:

- The partners have a covenant restricting involvement of each one in any other intimate relationships.
- The partners agree to avoid or limit thoughts, feelings, and actions related to emotional attachment or physical affection with others.
- The partners feel and express a sense of control over or ownership of almost all aspects of each other's intimate behavior.
- Each partner actively guards his/her "mate" to prevent overtures by outsiders toward the other partner.
- If there is a breach of the fidelity vow, this action will have serious consequences, including possibly, the termination of the relationship.

Possessive intimate relationships can, of course, be one-sided, as in those arrangements in which only one of the partners is limited and the other is not. The archetypal sheik and his harem, for example, may represent the most extreme type of possessive intimate relationship.

Possessive intimate relationships, including such double-standard arrangements, are well known and have existed for millennia. What is less well known is the relatively recent movement of some adventuresome people toward exploring the more open and consensual end of the possessive/non-possessive continuum.

With romantic couples, a possessive intimate relationship usually begins when the couple decides they want to move from just dating to some form of "commitment." Further deepening of the possessive aspects of the relationship generally occurs if the couple moves to being engaged and then married.

The terms of possessiveness are widely prevalent and explicit in our language and our cultural institutions. In wedding vows, for example, we commonly find the phrases "to have and to hold," "forsaking all others," and so on. Other possessive and restrictive language is ensconced in our laws referencing infidelity/adultery as grounds for divorce and other legal sanctions.

It's pretty clear that intimate relationships of the possessive variety are not only the norm in our contemporary Western culture but the standard adopted by all but a tiny minority of people across virtually all societies.

Those few exceptions in which non-possessive intimate relationships are not the social norm are so rare, crossculturally, as to attract the attention of anthropologists who may study their "deviant" relationship practices. Descriptions of these non-possessive societies are perused with amusement (and secret envy?) by sophisticated readers who may shake their heads at the immorality of these "primitives."

In our modern world, almost everyone is acculturated to establish and maintain possessive intimate relationships. While young people are usually given some leeway in terms of time and opportunities to explore various options, the expected goal is always, ultimately, to select a partner that one will possess and be possessed by.

Even the search process is generally considered to be appropriate only if it is structured as a series of monogamous relationships, each one ending before the next begins. Those individuals who may want to explore several intimate relationships simultaneously are often considered morally suspect.

Of course, double standards abound specifically here. Men may earn extra status points (at least among other envious males) for being able to juggle multiple female lovers concurrently. Women who maintain intimate relations with more than one man at a time are often tagged with derogatory labels, however.

For the most part, those couples and individuals who adopt a non-possessive intimate relationship orientation reject the monogamy-based concepts of strict fidelity demands, mate guarding, and the frequently associated double standards. They usually do so not because they are unable to comply with these exclusivist restrictions and societal proscriptions but because they are looking for a more adaptive love-style and especially one that better meets their needs.

Searching for the Best of Both Worlds

"It's never too late to have a happy childhood."[4]

—Tom Robbins

For most monogamous couples, a choice must be made between the benefits of having a stable, supportive relationship versus the benefits of having the freedom to engage with new sexual/romantic partners. This either/or dichotomy pits relationship security against erotic spontaneity. The epiphany that has come to most non-possessive couples is that this tug-of-war can be rejected as an unnecessary sacrifice of one or the other benefit.

The argument of the non-possessives is that by mutual agreement, and through good communication, honesty, and trust, an intimate relationship can be structured to allow for the best of both alternatives. Their insight is that the universal human dilemma of having to choose between security and stimulation can be resolved by a creative restructuring of the terms of the relationship.

Transitioning to a less possessive arrangement offers the possibility of maintaining a stable, supportive relationship while still being able to explore new intimacy possibilities. For non-possessive people, this restructuring of the primary relationship to include jointly consensual sex/romance with others is a preferred alternative to the customary options in a traditional relationship, such as suppression, covert affairs, divorce, and so on. Those choosing non-possessiveness usually view this approach as being upfront and honest, recognizing the needs of both partners and avoiding harm to others.

Unattached single individuals may have a lot of sexual intensity and variety in their lives but they most often lack the ongoing support and stability of a committed relationship. Long-term married couples may have solid support in their relationship but erotic intensity and variety may be lacking. The non-possessive option may allow for an elegant solution to these dilemmas by allowing for some time-sharing between these two relationship styles.

A significant number of couples discover the possibility of a non-possessive relationship as a mid-life revelation. Typically, these people have been married or in some other form of exclusive relationship for many years. As such, they approach the idea of openness with a fair amount of maturity and personal knowledge, both of themselves and of their primary partner.

One aspect of that maturity is the realization that, with time, passion may fade and the erotic attraction that was once there between the partners may no longer be as intense now. The rest of the relationship may be quite positive and their union may be mutually perceived as very much worth keeping.

Instead of making the baby/bathwater error, the couple may choose to explore non-possessive alternatives as a creative solution to meet otherwise unfulfilled needs. The insightful understanding here is that no relationship likely meets all needs at all times. Instead of settling for frustrations, blaming, and other expressions of unhappiness with each other, the couple may opt to outsource the fulfillment of these unmet desires.

In evolving their relationship into a non-possessive format, the partners in the couple may agree on a commitment to each other which includes all types of emotional support and intimacy but does not include a prohibition on sex with others. The range of what can be included in these non-exclusive agreements can be quite extensive.

The friends-with-benefits model, in which a person may be loosely connected to a network of social/sexual contacts but have no particular obligation to any specific other person, may illustrate one end of the non-possessive range of alternatives. At the other end of the scale are long-term married couples who commit to share everything together, including even their outside sexual partners.

One significant plus of opening up a relationship to the possibility of non-possessive options is the rediscovery of the joy of dating. Because of the traditional covenants regarding fidelity, most partners in a long-term exclusive relationship generally lose touch with what it was like to be single and available. The realization that they could experience this status again, even if only on a part-time basis, can be a revelation.

Many non-possessive couples were previously monogamous for some lengthy time since they first got together to go steady, get married, etc. Their non-monogamous activities now may represent a kind of return to a time when each was single and dating, only this time, they may be dating together as a couple.

Many of these couples express a sense of loss of the excitement from their single days. Their recreational sex adventures may now provide them with a way to recapture some of the thrill of dating, flirtation, seduction, and so on from the more youthful phase of their lives. This pattern appears to be especially prevalent among couples who married young.

Another common pattern among non-possessive couples is that in which each partner was quite sexually active with others before they got together and they simply agreed to continue these activities after they became a couple. In this scenario, the individuals involved may never have had a time in which they were completely monogamous.

For all types of non-possessive couples, there is a clear attempt to have the best of both worlds. The partners in a non-possessive relationship may each be free to expand their sexual/romantic horizons with outsiders and yet still have the security, support, and intimacy of a long-term partner's commitment. For couples who are successful with this having-your-cake-and-eating-it-too style, a fringe benefit is often much greater honesty, sensitivity, and communication in their primary relationship.

Keeping Love Alive

"Love is the greatest refreshment in life."[5]

—Picasso

Like a bonfire, love flares and then fades. This may be the single-most common observation of human nature, as documented by poets, novelists, songwriters, and others. The universal challenge of how to keep the love-flame burning has occupied our best creative minds for millennia but with relatively little agreement in the way of a solution.

In no other aspect of the relationship is the arcing trajectory of intensity over time seen more clearly than in the case of erotic passion. Newly-bonded partners may have difficulty keeping their hands off each other at the beginning of their relationship. As months and years go by, however, they may find they have difficulty generating enough enthusiasm for any sexual contact at all with each other.

A very common problem among couples who have been together for an extended time is how to remain passionate with each other. Over time in a relationship, not only do perceptions of desirability typically decline but so do flirtation/seduction/romance skill levels.

The partners of a long-term monogamous couple often lose the motivation to excite passion in each other and their abilities to attract and succeed with any sex partner may atrophy. Couples who transition to a non-possessive relationship, however, often report that one of the big benefits of this lifestyle change is the opportunity to practice (again) their flirting/seductive/romantic skills that may have become rusty with disuse.

Dressing provocatively, especially for women, talking seductively, especially for men, may make the partners in a long-term relationship feel younger and more alive again. Also, flirting/seductive behaviors can not only help the one engaging in these activities feel better about themselves, but seeing these actions in one's partner can help promote an improved image of that partner.

A husband's waning interest in his wife of several years may be recharged upon seeing her arouse sexual responsiveness in other males by her sexy clothes and provocative behavior. ("OMG, my wife is hot!") Similarly, a wife who may have come to take her husband for granted may view him with renewed interest after watching him successfully seduce other women at a swing party.

For many non-possessive couples, the opportunity to engage in conjointly approved sex with outsiders provides an excitement and stimulation that may be missing in an otherwise satisfying relationship. The chance to experience again the thrill of being sexually attractive to others may add a significant element of rejuvenation to a long-term relationship that may be stable but is less exciting now.

Among those who develop non-traditional intimate arrangements, a wide range of relationship styles may exist.

Some couples, for example, may have sex with each other but share little else. In these arrangements, the two people may relate more like single individuals but have an understanding that each is there for the other when one wants sex (and other options are not readily available). This type of relationship among heterosexuals is much like the well-known "bum buddy" pairings among gays.

Alternatively, a couple, married or not, may share the deepest of commitments to each other in every way but still be harmoniously open to having sex with others. These couples may be exclusive in all other aspects of their relationship, maintaining shared values, experiences, rituals, and possessions only between the two partners.

Such soulmates may be deeply in love with each other and have a long-standing bond of mutual support, caring, and sharing with only each other. Nevertheless, they find that they still want and need external sexual stimulation and they are able to successfully build that excitement into their relationship precisely because of their strong commitment to each other as a couple.

Most monogamous people (and most family therapists) generally believe that any relationship in which the partners have sex with others must be a fragile bonding that will likely be further weakened by continued outside sexual activity. To them, it is somewhat counterintuitive that this type of arrangement could actually strengthen the relationship.

It may be at least partly because of its rejuvenating effects that many non-possessive couples report that engaging in approved sex with others does, in fact, re-bond their union. Some, indeed, credit the move to more openness as saving their marriage.

Less dramatically, the most common report among successful non-possessive couples is that extracurricular erotic activities provide at least two very tangible benefits. Not only does this type of arrangement satisfy erotic needs that may otherwise be unfulfilled, but it may also, and more importantly, reignite passion between the primary partners.

Seeking Sexual Sensuousness

> "If it feels good, don't do it."
>
> —Puritan bumper sticker

Questions regarding the purpose of sex can be answered in many different ways. Those with the most traditional or conservative values might say that that procreation is the only valid reason to have sexual relations. Those with a "family values" perspective might add that the function of sex is also to promote bonding but only between a man and a woman who are married (to each other!).

On the more liberal (or libertine) end of the spectrum, sex may be regarded as one of life's great pleasures and as an activity that should be engaged in solely for its own sake with no extraneous purpose needed. Non-possessive people, for the most part, not only adopt this perspective but also make the search for sexual satisfaction into an art form, seeking to maximize pleasurable opportunities.

For many unattached individuals, especially single women, the purpose of dating is to identify and secure a potential mate. The sex that occurs during a dating relationship is often viewed as part of the broader testing of compatibility.

In addition to asking if we have the same likes in food, politics, and so on, each potential partner wants to know if we do well together in bed. If the erotic compatibility answers come up positive, a long-term committed relationship may look more promising.

For most couples, once the pair bonding is confirmed, there is no need to test compatibility with others and a possessive relationship is established. Intimate relations with others are suspended and the couple becomes exclusive.

For non-possessive couples, there is also no need to assess sexual compatibility with others as part of a mate-selection process. As they are no longer motivated by this need to use sex to find, test, and secure a long-term partner, couples in a less exclusive relationship are then free to explore sexual interactions with others primarily for the pleasures involved.

Because they have their primary bonding needs already met, the partners in a non-possessive couple have the option to become sexual hedonists and can focus on finding with others the most satisfying erotic experiences possible. Just as some people may develop high-level skills in the appreciation of fine food and wine, these couples may become connoisseurs of great sex.

The partners in these non-possessive relationships may seek and engage with those outsiders who are able to offer the very best erotic experiences. Travel to exotic/erotic locations and venues may be a part of this epicurean quest, much like more traditional couples may do wine-country tours or gourmet restaurant trips.

One of the appeals of the non-possessive lifestyle is the opportunity to engage in satisfying sex with others even if one is not maximally attractive. Although attractiveness is always a significant factor (for both genders) in sex playmate selection, there is a wider tolerance for and acceptance of the less physically appealing members in most of the non-possessive communities, as compared to the possessive dating scene, for example.

For those who may be a little older, a little overweight, or otherwise not quite ready for primetime on the model runway, the various non-possessive options may offer a way to still find satisfying sexual experiences, much more so than they may be able to achieve by searching for prospects in a pick-up bar, for example.

Many non-possessive adherents, who may not have washboard abs or porn star bodies, compensate by practicing and developing high-level erotic skills (for example, in the arts of oral pleasuring) which place them in high demand among the cognoscenti. ("Have you had a session with Randy/Randi yet? S/he has the most amazing mouth and tongue.")

There is even a bit of reverse snobbery seen directed at the "beautiful people" who may be regarded as poseurs. Those who look great but don't do much are often referred to as "Ken and Barbie" couples.

As in everything else, gender differences play a role in the search for sensuousness. Men's drive for sexual variety is well known but women, in spite of intense societal suppression and denial, have their own erotic desires and needs for satisfaction in this way also, of course.

Although it has been vehemently denied by the most conservative elements in our culture, many if not most women, if given the right opportunity, will actively embrace their sexual natures. These women may demand good sex and will respond positively to situations that allow them to express their sexuality in a safe, supported, and empowering environment.

Many women are, thus, attracted to non-possessive intimate relationships because they allow for some satisfaction of their strongly felt urges for sensuality. Contrary to the culturally proscribed focus on the search for the perfect husband, these women want to feel sexually alive in the present moment. Instead of looking for Mr. Right, they are more concerned with finding Mr. Right Now.

Avoiding the Pitfalls of Possessiveness

When Mose Allison sings, "I'm sittin' in here for the rest of my life, and all I did was shoot my wife,"[6] he so perfectly expresses the righteous indignation that often accompanies jealous violence.

Non-possessive adherents not only embrace this relationship lifestyle for its positive benefits but many also do it to make a statement against what they see as the potentially destructive effects of possessive relationships. As an example, they may point to the horrific violence perpetrated against others by jealous lovers who feel they have been wronged.

When possessive arrangements between or among people are going well, these relationships can provide many benefits to the partners. People involved in exclusive unions often report positive feelings as a result of not sharing intimacies with outsiders. Commonly described positives include a sense of satisfaction derived from committing one's total fidelity/loyalty to another person and receiving the same total commitment from them.

Exclusive forms of relationships, in which each partner exerts some control over or possession of their partner's intimate behavior, may work well if needs are met for each by this arrangement. The problems arise, however, when one or both partners feel that desires, wishes, and wants are not being satisfied and/or the relationship is not going well.

A rational response to unmet needs might involve a search for alternate forms of the relationship that could be more satisfying. Unfortunately, when faced with dissatisfaction in a possessive arrangement, most people tend to be more emotional than logical.

When discontent arises, a typical response among those who have a strong need to control the behavior of others is to "double down" on the possessive aspects of the relationship. Restrictions on the activities of the partner may increase, suspicions regarding their compliance may surface, and distrust may poison the relationship.

Jealousy, of course, is the biggest negative consequence of possessive arrangements. Romantic jealousy is unique in that it only occurs when someone feels that someone they believe they own may be taken away from them by someone else.

That peculiar emotional response we call "jealousy" is actually a combination of anxiety and anger. Faced with a potential loss, the possessor understandably feels anxious as they contemplate continuing without their loved one. In jealousy, anxiety and anger are combined with a suspicious mindset, resulting in guarding behaviors involving the love object.

Whereas anxiety is an inner-directed emotion, anger is most often directed outward toward others in the form of hostile behavior. Possessive partners may attempt to engage in aggressive actions against the rival whom they believe is attempting to steal their loved one away from them. As an indication of the intensity of these possessive rages, the one who feels the jealousy may also direct their hostility toward the loved partner who has presumably allowed this threat to occur.

Hostile retaliations on the part of jealous lovers are, of course, extremely common in virtually all cultures and evidently have been the norm in almost all of recorded history. (Google "the cuckold's revenge.")

In today's news, one can hardly scan any popular media content without encountering at least one story describing some kind of violence being perpetrated by someone in a jealous rage. Assaults and murders are carried out not only victimizing the alleged interloper but also inflicted, at times, on the presumed wayward partner.

Reliable data regarding the extent of jealousy-fueled violence are hard to come by. Just extrapolating from anecdotal reports in news feeds, however, every year there must be many thousands of serious injuries and deaths attributable to the s(he)-done-me-wrong revenge motive.

Tales of the jealous lover extracting retribution against his rival and the unfaithful partner have been plot staples since the dawn of literature and continue to the present time to create a whole genre of books, plays, films, etc., with this theme. Authors, playwrights, and screenwriters have mined this rich vein of human passion from Homer through Shakespeare to Maya Angelou.

Sensationalized accounts of violence arising from jealousy continue to fascinate the general public. (Witness the infamous "Trial of the Century" involving a certain Mr. Simpson.)

Taming the Rage Reaction

"Can't we all just get along?"[7]

—Rodney King

In our culture, we may believe that we abhor violence and we may think that our criminal justice system is diligent in meting out sanctions to punish attacks against others, regardless of motives. When it comes to cases involving jealous rage, however, there is a curious exception.

Most judges and juries are willing to grant some leeway in finding against someone who may be considered to have used force to defend their personal property from intrusions by an outsider. This type of leniency may be extended from tangible goods to one's relationship partner.

Much like the exemptions granted to homeowners who may shoot an intruder with impunity, the violently jealous may be granted a kind of "hall pass" from prosecution if they are perceived to be only attempting to protect their intimate "possession." As a result of these sympathetic attitudes, some of which are ensconced in various statutes, "crimes of passion" may be lightly punished, if at all.

A vicious cycle may be in play here if potential perpetrators of jealous aggression realize they may be able to get away with it by mounting the wronged-spouse defense. Rather than being blinded by justifiable rage, as defense attorneys would like jurors to believe, these perpetrators may have weighed their options in a more premeditated manner.

Consistent with their natural role as the most violent of the genders, men are by far the most frequent perpetrators of jealous aggression. Not to be outdone, however, women excel in evolving more creative ways to achieve parity in the matter of expressing jealous rage. (See the many creative works based on William Congreve's famous quote, "Hell hath no fury. . . ."[8])

The net effect of current social and legal attitudes toward jealous aggression is to reinforce the standard model of possessive relationships. Woe be it to anyone who might intrude upon an existing possessive intimate relationship. Extreme caution may be necessary lest the intruder become a victim of righteous retaliation.

At least partly as a consequence, many non-possessive people deliberately structure their relationships to avoid, or at least minimize, the destructive effects of jealousy. By allowing their loved one the freedom to engage intimately with others and by learning to control negative thoughts and feelings when these do occur, these non-possessive lovers are able to steer clear of the worst ravages of jealousy.

Using an approach based more on self-control, rather than the control of others, the partners of these non-possessive couples are able to spare themselves the anxiety and anger associated with attempts at monopolizing their loved one's affections. In addition, they also avoid potential repercussions associated with hostile behavior toward outsiders and each other.

By not insisting upon complete control over the intimate behavior of their spouse, for example, a husband or wife may find more peace within themselves and a better relationship with that spouse. Non-possessive couples often report a sense of relief if they are able to give up the drama associated with attempting to enforce and comply with the demands of sexual fidelity.

Most non-possessive couples are decidedly apolitical regarding their chosen lifestyle. Nevertheless, many view themselves as setting an example of how people could or should relate to each other positively to avoid the destructive effects of jealous rage.

Going Underground in a Vanilla World

"Take a walk on the wild side."[9]

—Lou Reed

Non-possessive couples are very aware that sexual play with others remains a significant taboo in the eyes of mainstream morality. As a result, their extramural activities are most often concealed from public view or disclosure.

Recreational sex clubs often have unlisted locations, ads requesting others who want to hook-up may be coded, and, to hide their identity, couples may adopt play-name aliases. (For some reason, "Thumper and Bambi" have become quite popular.)

All of this creates a sort of underground subculture and those who are involved in it often experience some satisfaction in being part of a "secret" society. (Although, from most accounts, the society meetings tend to be a lot more fun than those held by the Elks Club.)

Perhaps more similar to the Masons, those involved in the recreational sex scene, for example, get together on a regular basis, use code words, and keep each other's identity confidential. (Their greetings tend to be a little more intimate than a secret handshake, however.)

Virtually all non-possessive couples need to maintain a "straight" image to present to most of the traditional world. Because consensual sex with other couples is still a major kapu in mainstream society, non-possessive couples generally do not reveal the nature of their covert activities to outsiders who may sanction them.

Just like a group of business and professional people who may like to dress up in leathers and ride their Harleys together on the weekends, these recreational-sex couples dress up in their play clothes and ride with each other in a way they find more stimulating.

Dressing up, in fact, is a very popular activity among those in the rec sex underground culture. Almost all clubs and travel events have many nights in which costumes are recommended or even required. These cosplay events allow non-possessive attendees to engage in a little role playing and reinforce the taking on of alternate personas (for example, the naughty schoolgirl and the principal).

Putting on their "club clothes" and adopting their play names permits the participants to explore multiple (and more erotic) personalities that may need to be suppressed during more quotidian activities. It can be like Halloween every weekend for some active players.

Some attendees revel in the costuming aspects almost exclusively and rarely participate in any actual sexual activities. Because these couples just like to strut around and display their colorful costumes, the more active participants often refer to them by mildly derogatory terms, such as "peacocks" or "sparkle ponies."

Our mainstream, traditional culture tends to disapprove of any sort of deviance from generally accepted mores. This disapproval is especially acute if the deviant behavior includes sex. As a result, most non-possessive couples become somewhat closeted, hiding their nonconforming behavior from those who may censure them.

These couples are careful not to come out of the non-possessive closet or to out others, as significant punitive consequences can occur. Most non-monogamous couples can report instances in which they have experienced negative gossip, avoidance by former friends, censure by family members, or even loss of employment following indiscreet disclosure of their "deviant" activities.

Consequently, most non-possessive couples lead a kind of double-identity life, perhaps appearing as a typical neighborhood husband and wife most of the time but, at other times, covertly morphing into lusty seekers of conjointly-approved, extra-relationship sex.

In situations in which mainstream society holds punitive power over a subgroup it views as deviant, the members of that group often develop denigrating attitudes toward that society. Among themselves, non-possessive couples generally refer to traditional couples using the mildly derogatory term "vanilla."

The obvious analogy is that the strictly monogamous couples never sample the other flavors of the ice-cream palate. (What, no Cherry Garcia!?)

Tweaking Family Values

"The family that plays together stays together."

—Mother Teresa[10]

Many non-possessive couples experience a sense of satisfaction in being part of a kind of sexual freedom counterculture. Along with the titillation of doing something that most others would deem as naughty, many non-possessive couples often feel a sense of superiority vis-à-vis the *Leave It to Beaver* portrayals of how a family should behave. Those who participate in partner-approved, extra-relationship sex frequently view themselves as more hip, edgy, and avant-garde than the vanilla population.

An especially sensitive aspect of the double-identity lifestyle is the matter of disclosure to family members. For example, most middle-aged, non-possessive couples don't tell their parents or other older relatives who are typically more conservative. For many younger couples, however, their parents may have come of age during the 1960s and '70s. These parents may have sexual attitudes that are considerably more liberal and they may be able to view atypical lifestyle choices more tolerantly.

Disclosure to adult children is another issue fraught with delicate choices. For many non-possessive parents, telling the grown kids about Mom and Dad's kinky lifestyle may earn status points for the parents, assuming the younger generation is more sexually liberal.

For non-possessive couples of the boomer generation, however, an inversion of values may exist. In many of these families, the children may be (much) more conservative than their parents. Revelations of unorthodox sexual relationships by Mom and Dad may be met with disbelief and chagrin as generations X, Y, and Millennial roll their eyes at the weirdness of their parents. (There must be enough material for a TV sitcom in this premise.)

Few non-possessive couples choose to disclose their activities to their younger children. (This may require explaining why Mommy and Daddy are dressing up so strangely and telling the babysitter that they won't be back until very late.)

Some couples attempt to explain, justify and promote their unconventional activities to their older children, often with mixed results. ("OMG, my parents are freaks!") In the service of passing on their freedom-based values, some parents even allow their much older children to observe some limited non-monogamous interactions.

At a more extreme level of parent-child activity sharing, there have been a few cases reported in which a mother and her adult daughter regularly go out to rec-sex events together. (Sort of a twist on "Take Your Kid to Work Day," this combination presents an interesting opportunity for the lucky guy who may get to do a threesome with both mother and daughter.)

The fact that some parents might want to introduce their adult children into the non-possessive relationship subculture illustrates how strongly positive many of these couples feel about their unconventional activities. In the view of many recreational-sex couples, their chosen lifestyle reflects some of the best virtues of human interaction. These couples point to such core values as honest communication and sensitivity to the needs of your loved one and see these as benefits of this lifestyle that they would like to foster in their kids.

Some couples can become active proselytizers, spreading the gospel of non-monogamy and attempting to persuade the vanilla people to give up the evils of jealousy and sexual possessiveness. So far, the mainstream culture appears resoundingly unconvinced and the recreational-sex religion will likely remain underground for some time. (For a darker outcome of this scenario, read *Stranger in a Strange Land*.[11])

Lacking the organization of the gay and lesbian subculture, there has not been a recreational-sex liberation movement, as yet. There have been, however, a few "Swinger Pride" marches, (with police escorts, no less!) especially in New Orleans during lifestyle conventions there. These events appear to function mainly as in-group solidarity boosters and likely have little effect on the curious and puzzled onlookers who probably regard them as just another of the wild and crazy things that happen in the Big Easy.

As another example of how involved in the non-monogamous lifestyle and how positive some couples are about the virtues of non-possessiveness, there have been more than a few marriages at recreational-sex clubs. With the wedding ceremony and the reception attended by a large number of friends (with benefits), this type of event illustrates how much bonding there is within these relatively tight-knit communities.

On a lighter note, during the post-reception party, one could imagine a whole new meaning to the playing of the traditional song, "Here Comes the Bride."

Navigating Changes

"We do not change as we grow older; we just become more clearly ourselves."[12]

—Lynn Hall

Couples that start having agreed-upon sexual encounters with outsiders generally find that these new activities alter their relationship in several ways. Many of these changes are complex and subtle, with some being perceived as positive and some negative.

Conjointly agreeing to engage sexually with others presents a whole series of challenges to the customary ways that traditional couples think, feel, and act. On the positive side, negotiating these changes often forces the couple to learn and utilize more effective relationship skills.

As an example, the initial process of agreeing on the specifics of when, where, and with whom to engage usually requires the partners of the couple to communicate clearly regarding their preferences, limitations, etc. Enhanced communication is one of the positive relationship changes most frequently cited by couples who have transitioned from a traditional to a less possessive arrangement.

Many couples report that having practiced and learned to communicate openly and honestly with each other about having sex with others, they can now more easily discuss other potentially sensitive topics. Issues that may have been avoided previously, or only dealt with obliquely, may not seem so threatening now.

Assertiveness skills often show improvement when couples move toward a non-possessive relationship style. The members of couples that engage in consensual sex with outsiders often comment that they are more comfortable identifying how they feel and in conveying this in a straightforward way to their primary partner.

Honesty is usually highly valued among non-possessive couples and most report that the avoidance of deception is a significant positive development that occurs in the transition from pre- to post-engagement with others. Again, this change is seen as a benefit that generalizes to other areas of the relationship.

Overall, couples that participate in primary-partner-approved sex with outsiders regard themselves as better able to talk about other sensitive issues than they were able to when they were strictly monogamous. Simply put, the members of most non-possessive couples seem to find that once they can master honest and assertive communication with each other regarding sex with outsiders, they can talk openly about anything.

Many couples that have successfully transitioned to a non-possessive relationship comment that there seems to be less emotional conflict in the relationship now as compared to when they were sexually exclusive. They often describe the process of engaging sexually with outsiders as one of learning to control strong negative feelings, such as jealousy, anger, anxiety, and so on.

Again, for many couples, this learned control seems to generalize to other negative emotions and these couples report less drama overall in their relationship than previously. In simple terms, a husband or wife who can watch her/his spouse have great sex with someone else without getting upset can probably accept a lot of other behaviors more calmly.

Not all changes reported by couples moving toward non-possessiveness are positive, however. Abandoning sexual exclusivity can cause both predictable and unexpected stresses in the relationship, which, if unresolved, may harm or even destroy the couple's primary bonding.

Among the negatives mentioned by couples newly experiencing non-possessive adventures is a certain loss of innocence. Once a couple involves themselves in agreed-upon extra-relationship sex, they can never again recapture the purity of exclusiveness. Lost are the romantic ideals of the one-and-only, the true love, etc., at least in terms of the sexual aspects of the relationship.

There is a very obvious parallel here with the Garden of Eden mythology. Once they have tasted the forbidden fruit of consensual sex with others, the couple can no longer return to the idyllic state of, "There's never been anyone else but you." It's no accident that many rec-sex lifestyle organizations (such as NASCA) use logos portraying an apple with a bite out of it.

For most couples that become involved in non-possessive activities, however, the loss of innocence issue does not appear to be a significant concern. Many of these couples are older, have relationships that are no longer new, and the partners tend to be quite experienced sexually. For them, the transition to non-monogamy does not pose any fall-from-grace images. Instead, they can identify some salacious pleasure in embracing the "sinful" nature of the act.

Non-possessive arrangements are relatively rare for couples who are very young and/or less experienced sexually. This is especially true among couples for whom this is their first significant relationship and for whom their bonding is still fresh.

There seems to be some degree of maturity (in several senses of that term) required before conjoint extracurricular activity is considered. When it does occur, it is often perceived as a kind of loss of virginity for the couple's relationship.

Although some non-possessive couples may find that they are perfectly compatible in terms of their interests, limitations, etc., regarding outside involvements, most struggle, at least somewhat, to resolve differing preferences and concerns. If the male and female partners in the couple have widely divergent needs and expectations regarding how much sex with whom and where and when, these disagreements can cause stresses that did not exist when the couple was monogamous.

Failure to find solutions to these differing viewpoints can, at times, cause the couple to revisit exclusivity, which may be perceived as a simpler way to avoid conflict. Other couples see the incompatibility as evidence that the relationship is not meeting their needs and start to consider alternatives.

Growing Older Gracefully

When Bob Dylan sang, "I was so much older then: I'm younger than that now,"[13] we recognized that, although we may age chronologically, we can adopt more youthful attitudes along the way. Dylan's lyrics resonate with many non-possessive couples who express the conviction that freeing up one's intimate relationship can lead to a rejuvenation of thoughts, feelings, and actions.

Everyone ages and everyone must find ways to cope with the inevitable decrements that come with the passing of years. Compared to those in exclusive relationships, non-possessive people often find they must face different challenges as they grow older. Their strategies to cope with aging are often significantly different also from those of their more traditional relationship-oriented age-peers.

Sexual and romantic attractiveness, as well as interest and performance capabilities, vary inversely with age. For long-term monogamous couples, these declines, although depressing perhaps, are often not a significant issue because they are not actively dating in any way.

For non-possessive couples, however, attractiveness and performance skills are essential for success in interacting intimately with external prospects. As non-monogamous couples get older, they may find that they are less successful, and subsequently less involved, in encounters with outsiders.

Issues of self-image may have to be resolved and compromises made. A common scenario is that of the somewhat-past-their-prime couple who are still looking for the young and beautiful people to hook up with but are now having less and less success. This pattern is similar to that seen in older gays, who date within a culture that places extreme value on youth and appearance.

This downward slide may be especially acute for the getting-older non-possessive couples. Some who been in this lifestyle for many years have invested a great deal of their self-image in being attractive to others. Rejection by those they still find appealing may elicit a denial defense. (An older couple may be overheard grousing that they don't want to hang around with a bunch of old people.)

Because they are not active in the dating marketplace, either individually or together, aging monogamous couples usually have less invested in looking attractive and may frequently neglect their appearance. In general, older non-possessive men and women tend to place a higher value on physical fitness, personal hygiene, and dressing well than their same-age monogamous counterparts.

With their above-average concern for maintaining at least the appearance of youthfulness as long as possible, aging non-possessive couples may be subject to the same identity stresses as individuals experiencing the commonly observed "mid-life crisis." Instead of focusing on the acquisition of material goods to bolster a feeling of still being young, however, non-possessive couples are more likely to emphasize the (re)learning of youthful behaviors, such as taking up active sports, practicing new dance steps, dressing fashionably, and more.

As a result, non-possessive couples often report that their involvement in primary-partner approved sex with external people has helped them look and feel much younger than they used to be when they were strictly monogamous. Perhaps attempting to validate the adage that you're only as old as you feel, then to some extent, these couples have been able to stave off at least some of the inevitable psychological effects of ageing by their choice of this unconventional lifestyle.

Some age-related stresses appear to be coming more prominent, however, within the non-possessive subculture. There is a large, older cohort of early adherents who have been involved for several decades now and are still interested in being active. They are being supplanted, to some extent, by a growing number of younger people who have discovered the joy of (non-possessive) sex only in the last several years.

This demographic split has led to some instances of ageism. The older folks have no problem, of course, partying with the neo-swing youngsters.

The reverse is not true, however. The "club kids" do not want to associate with anyone who might remind them of their parents. ("OMG, Jeremy, that woman who was coming on to you looks just like your mother!")

Some rec-sex clubs and other venues have adopted age-tiered events with age-appropriate music to match, such as Saturday nights for the hip-hop crew and Sunday afternoons for the oldies-but-goodies set. Whereas previously one could show up at any time, now it pays to read the program of events to avoid the embarrassment of getting in with the wrong crowd.

Definitions of "too old" vary, of course, (especially as one ages!). Also, intimate events that may be described as more appropriate for one age group or the other rarely specify just what age is considered the cut-off point. Among the young Turks of both genders, however, there is somewhat of a consensus that if you're over 40, you're over the hill.

Some clubs and other venues have recently started to enforce age restrictions. A few market themselves as for the young only and, as private social meeting places, they are able to be choosy and achieve success in creating a youthful clientele.

Membership applications may require recently-dated photos and birthdate verification. Social networking pages may be scrutinized to check for interests/activities/friends deemed to be too mature. ("What, you're not on Facebook, don't tweet, and don't text with your thumbs on your smart phone? Don't even think about applying.")

For the most part, these organizations are successful in bringing together groups of smooth-skinned 20- and 30-somethings and screening out anybody with wrinkles.

Coping with Dissolution

"There is no remedy for love but to love more."[14]

—Henry David Thoreau

Like all relationships, non-possessive unions wax and wane, following various trajectories of strength of intimacy. The initial infatuation inevitably gives way to decreasing intensity and/or a stabilizing adjustment between the partners. (Familiarity may not breed contempt but it most often breeds complacency.)

Non-possessive relationships do not appear to be any more or less vulnerable to dissolution than monogamous relationships but are affected by somewhat different stresses and strengths. Again, there are similarities to the civil unions of gay and lesbian couples.

Having sex with people outside the primary partnership, even if consensually agreed to, may create unexpected strains in the relationship. Strong feelings of jealousy, anger, abandonment fears, and other negative emotions may be covert initially but may emerge at flash points to be serious risks to the continuation of the relationship.

On the other hand, many non-possessive couples seem to find a certain strength in their atypical type of relationship. Some find that the sexual freedom inherent in their arrangement works actually as a form of commitment to each other. (e.g., "I love you so much because you allow me to explore my wildest desires in a way that few other partners would.")

Non-possessive couples in which the partners are deeply bonded emotionally to each other are able to engage in sex with outsiders with less risk to the relationship largely because of the partner's trust in each other. Extramural intimacies may become a validation of the strength of their union. ("We love each other so much, we can even have sex with other people and it doesn't diminish our relationship. See how strong we are together.")

In monogamous relationships, sexual fidelity is usually understood to be one of the most critical shared values and often is even the defining element binding the partners together. In non-monogamous arrangements, the partners generally seek and find other core values, such as emotional intimacy, mutual support, shared history, and so on, on which to base their primary relationship.

Because the prohibition regarding sex with others is so vitally important to most monogamous relationships, infidelity can be a very serious problem to those involved. When, for example, one member of a monogamous couple is discovered to be having a covert affair, this discovery typically creates a significant challenge to the relationship and can frequently result in its breakup.

Because sexual fidelity is not the primary shared value between/among those involved in non-possessive arrangements, transgressions (however defined) are much less likely to result in serious conflict, unresolved stress, or rupture of the relationship. Couples adopting the non-possessive alternative often report that their primary relationship is more stable as a result of this transition to non-monogamy, because a lot of drama regarding the sexual fidelity issue is removed.

A couple that is involved in swinging, for example, is unlikely to break up because one partner has sex, even if not agreed upon, with somebody else. Compared to monogamous couples, the commonplace cause and effect of adultery leading to divorce is a much less likely outcome for the non-possessive couple.

Stresses surrounding sexual activity with others can and do occur, of course, in non-possessive relationships as well. In virtually all of these non-exclusive arrangements, there are some agreements as to limits on external sexual activity. Conflicts may arise when one person in the relationship is viewed as violating those agreements. Although these conflicts can be significant, they rarely rise to the level seen in monogamous relationships when sexual boundaries with others are exceeded.

When monogamous relationships come apart, especially due to sexual infidelity, the former partners are frequently quite hostile to each other with recriminations commonly involving accusations of deceit, betrayal, etc. When the partners in a non-possessive arrangement find themselves moving toward dissolution of the relationship, the process can often be a lot more respectful, cordial, and even supportive.

For many traditional couples, especially those who are married, a breakup of the monogamous relationship is particularly traumatic because the partners typically have invested so many of their needs (for example, social, financial, sexual) into the failed partnership. On the other hand, the partners involved in non-possessive arrangements may sort of hedge their bets in terms of getting their needs met by developing auxiliary or complementary relationships outside the primary commitment.

In a monogamous couple, if one of the partners moves to break up that relationship, this action can often leave the remaining partner with few remaining support systems. In a non-possessive breakup, each of the previous primary partners generally has at least a few options to get some of their basic sexual or emotional needs met through the existing intimate relationships they may have already established with others.

For some non-possessive persons, such as those involved in polyamory arrangements, several close friends/lovers may become a kind of extended family. In these intimate social networks, breakups are even less of an issue, as it expected that primary coupling may shift and evolve within the group.

A non-possessive couple may decide together that they no longer want to consider their relationship as primary and each of them may want to explore developing a new primary relationship with someone else or just remain uncommitted for a while. Because of their non-possessive attitude, this transition can be jointly embraced and the partners can maintain the remaining positive aspects of their relationship without the need for blaming or any other relationship-destroying hostilities.

Many formerly-bonded non-possessive partners who have separated are thus able to continue a warm and positive relationship with their ex. Surprisingly to some, this continuation can often include sex. (See Meryl Streep in *It's Complicated*[15] for an amusing riff on this scenario.)

As compared to the clichéd request of traditional partners who are separating ("Can't we still be friends?"), separating non-possessive partners are more likely to ask, "Can't we still be lovers?"

Pursuing Happiness

"He who binds himself to a joy
Does the winged life destroy:
But he who kisses the joy as it flies
Lives in eternity's sunrise."[16]

—William Blake

Monogamous couples who are considering the switch to a non-possessive form of their relationship often ruminate over whether this transition will result in a happy ending (figuratively or literally). They want to know if those people who are involved in the various non-possessive lifestyles are any more satisfied with their choice than their more conservative counterparts.

In terms of the risk of unhappy endings, the few studies of non-possessive intimate relationships that have been reported appear to indicate that couples with less exclusive arrangements are neither more nor less likely to terminate their partnership than those with traditional relationships.[17]

In general, these reports suggest that the divorce rate among married couples who define themselves as swingers, polyamorous, and the like is about the same as that for couples who are strictly monogamous. These studies have limited credibility, however, because of multiple methodological problems, including those in the areas of subject selection, response bias, and outcome measurement.

In terms of expressed satisfaction with their relationship, traditional couples as a group may be seen as clustering around the midpoint on the happiness/unhappiness scale, with a fairly wide range of tapering dispersion in both the positive and negative directions—that is, a somewhat "normal" distribution.

Anecdotal observations of couples in non-possessive intimate relationships suggest that their distribution on the satisfaction scale may be more bimodal, however. Among those in non-possessive relationships, there appears to be a "happy" cluster at one end and an "unhappy" cluster at the other end of the continuum of contentedness.

A significant subset of the overall population of couples involved in non-possessive intimate relationships appears to be quite pleased with their nontraditional lifestyle. They report that their non-monogamous arrangement strengthens their bonding with each other and is a source of significant satisfaction for them. Although not without its challenges, for these couples, permitting erotic and/or romantic engagements with others seems to provide more benefits than costs.

Many of these "happy" couples describe how they feel like they have achieved the best of both worlds—the benefits of being married plus the perks of acting single. They present as successful and confident in their relationship and pleased that they have discovered and adopted a lifestyle that suits their values and their personalities.

These satisfied non-possessive couples report that they have been able to discover and implement an innovative way to balance their needs for competing factors, such as risk and reward, excitement and security, novelty and stability, etc.

These couples are quite gratified that they made the decision to make their relationship less possessive and would not want to return to having a more restrictive, monogamous-style arrangement.

At the other end of the satisfaction continuum, however, there appears to be a cluster of couples that are relatively unhappy with their choice of a non-possessive arrangement in their relationship. For this group, erotic and/or romantic activities with persons outside the partnership appear to create more stress than pleasure. This "unhappy" cluster of couples may express a lack of trust, confidence, and more in themselves and/or each other and may report communication difficulties.

In one common sequence of events, a couple who may view their traditional arrangement as lacking in sufficient satisfaction may try to use non-possessiveness as a solution to "save" the relationship. This unfortunate strategy is similar, of course, to that of the couple that is unhappy together and as a result of this unhappiness, decides to have a child in an attempt to save their marriage. In each case, the new demands, rather than bringing the couple closer, add more stress and potential conflict, often leading to the breakup of the relationship.

Another common variant observed among couples experiencing discontent in their exploration of non-possessive arrangements is that in which one of the partners is very enthusiastic about engaging erotically with outsiders and the other partner is not. In this situation, the enthusiastic partner may convince the reluctant one to try sex with others and significant negative feelings may result, often for both partners, sometimes leading to the dissolution of the relationship.

A somewhat ironic twist in this scenario is seen, at times, when the enthusiastic partner (typically the male) finally convinces the reluctant partner (typically the female) to try sex with others. After a few experiences, the roles become reversed when she finds she *really* likes it and demands a lot more, causing some consternation on the part of the male who wonders what Pandora's box he has opened.

This phenomenon is common enough to be a source of amusement among experienced non-possessive couples, as they chuckle at the somewhat predictable "newbie switcheroo." We are again reminded of the old adage, "Be careful what you wish for."

Loving Non-Possessively

John Lennon challenged us to, "Imagine no possessions; I wonder if you can."[18] Inherent in this directive is the understanding that, for almost all of us, possessions are an integral part of our lives and it's almost impossible to imagine a life without them.

As with any alternative lifestyle, there are those non-possessive couples that see their atypical relationship form as a model for others and that view themselves as in the vanguard of a social movement dedicated to the eradication of the evils of monogamy. They attempt to spread the doctrine that if everyone would just love non-possessively, the world would be a much happier place.

Aside from a few open-lifestyle evangelicals, however, most couples who are already participants generally agree that non-possessive intimate relationships are not for everyone. In fact, the consensus seems to be that non-monogamous relationships may be appropriate only for a small minority of couples.

The stresses, both personal and interpersonal, of managing a non-possessive relationship plus the psychological demands necessary to succeed may not make this type of arrangement workable for most people. In spite of our avowed reverence for life, liberty, and the pursuit of happiness, the costs of non-conformity, especially to strongly-held sexual/religious values, are high in our culture.

Nevertheless, for those couples, however limited their number may be, who do have the personal qualities to make it work, the non-possessive option appears to be a very adaptive lifestyle choice. The partners of these couples appear to have found an innovative way of relating to each other and to outsiders that amounts to a sort of win-win-win outcome.

The partners involved in such relationships have been able to uncouple sex, and in some cases romance and even love, from the primary bonds that hold them together. For the successful couples, the results of this choice have been not only positive but transformative. In most cases, their non-possessive style has enabled them to meet several previously unfulfilled needs and even to create greater bonding between the partners.

The success of some, however, should not be taken as a prescription for all. For many people, and especially for bonded couples, attempting to transition into a non-possessive relationship may be fraught with pitfalls.

It has not been the intent of this survey and analysis to promote or advocate for non-possessive intimate relationships. Nor has it been the purpose of this review to argue against them.

The purpose of this overview has simply been to objectively describe the benefits as well as the risks of these types of arrangements, to examine the factors which predispose people to choose them, and to explain how these relationships work, psychologically, for those who make this decision.

For the couple that is considering adding an element of non-possessiveness to their relationship, the best advice is to proceed slowly in small increments, testing reactions at each step. Moving too quickly can unleash unexpected feelings, thoughts, and behaviors.

Although the joys of non-possessive intimate relationships may beckon, the hazards may not be apparent initially. Proceeding cautiously is prudent until it is certain that, in exploring this new form of relating to each other, both partners continue to share the trust, honesty, and good communication that bind the couple together.

When that certainty is present, however, the non-possessive approach to intimate relationships can offer a novel and productive alternative for those willing and able to make it work.

If this is you, enjoy!

Notes

Chapter 1. Intimate Relationships

1. Cramer, T. (1928). *The Book of Common Prayer*. Cambridge: Cambridge University Press.

2. O'Neill, N. & O'Neill, G. (1972). *Open Marriage*. New York: Lippincott.

3. Barker, M. & Langdridge, D., eds. (2010). *Understanding Non-Monogamies*. London: Routledge.

4. Marlowe, C. (1590). *The Passionate Shepherd to His Love*. Retrieved from *Poets.org*. Accessed Jan. 1, 2017.

5. Jobim, A. C. (1962). *The Girl from Ipanema*. Santa Monica, CA: Universal Music Group.

6. Whitehead, A. N. (1919). *The Concept of Nature*. Salt Lake City, UT: Project Gutenberg.

7. Reich, W. (2013 [newly translated]). *The Sexual Revolution*. New York: Macmillan.

8. Newton, I. (1687). *Laws of Motion*. London: S. Pepys.

9. Lyne, A. (Director). (1986). *9½ Weeks*. Hollywood: Warner Brothers.

10. Cianfrance, D. (Director). (2010). *Blue Valentine*. Hollywood: Weinstein Company

11. Reiner, R. (Director). (1989). *When Harry Met Sally*. Hollywood: Columbia Pictures.

12. DeVito, D. (Director). (1989). *War of the Roses*. Hollywood: 20th Century Fox.

13. Hupfeld, H. (1931). *As Time Goes By*. Los Angeles: Warner Brothers.

14. Mead, M. (1928). *Coming of Age in Samoa*. New York: William Morrow.

15. DeMaria, R. (1978). *Communal Love at Oneida*. New York: Edwin Mellen Press.

16. Gold, H. (1971). *The Sexual Freedom League*. Paris: Olympia Press.

17. Ellis, A. (1971). *The Civilized Couple's Guide to Extramarital Adventure*. New York: Pinnacle.

18. Taylor, E. & Sharkey, L. (2006). *Em & Lo's Rec Sex.* San Francisco: Chronicle Books.

19. De Vega, L. (1613). *Fuenteovejuna* in (1962). Flores, A., editor. *Great Spanish Plays in English.* New York: Dover Publications.

Chapter 2. Non-Exclusive Arrangements

1. Chopra, D. (2003). *The Spontaneous Fulfillment of Desire.* New York: Harmony.

2. Frost, R. (1916). *The Road Not Taken.* New York: Holt.

3. Camus, A. (1972). *La Mort Heureuse.* Paris: Gallimard.

4. Brown, R. (1974). "Sexual Arousal, the Coolidge Effect and Dominance in the Rat." *Animal Behavior* (22) 634–37.

5. Carroll, L. (1865). *Alice's Adventures in Wonderland.* Seattle: Amazon Books.

Chapter 3. Non-Possessive Relationship Issues

1. Shakira. (2001). *Underneath Your Clothes.* Los Angeles: EMI Music.

2. Mead, M. (1928). *Coming of Age in Samoa.* New York: William Morrow.

3. Malinowski, B. (1929). *The Sexual Life of Savages.* San Francisco: Internet Archive.

4. Reich, W. (1931). *The Invasion of Compulsory Sex Morality.* New York: Farrar.

5. Shakespeare, W. (1603). *The Tragedy of Othello.* London: Iaggard and Blunt.

6. Ryan, C. & Jetha, C. (2010). *Sex at Dawn.* New York: Harper Collins.

7. Shakespeare, W. (1603). *All's Well That Ends Well.* London: Iaggard and Blunt.

8. Dylan, B. (1966). *Absolutely Sweet Marie.* New York: Columbia Recorda.

9. Perel, E. (2006). *Mating In Captivity.* New York: Harper.

10. Turner, T. (1984). *What's Love Got To Do With It?* Los Angeles: RPM.

11. Stewart, P. (1964). *Jacobellis v. Ohio.* U.S. Supreme Court.

12. Burns, G. & Allen, G. (1937). *The Burns and Allen Show.* New York: NBC.

13. von Trier, L. (2013). *Nymphomania.* Copenhagen: Les Films du Losange.

14. Joplin, J. (1971). *Me and Bobby McGee.* Los Angeles: BNA.

15. Cantor, E. (1928). *Makin' Whoopee.* New York: RCA Victor.

16. Stills, S. (1970). *Love the One You're With.* Los Angeles: Atlantic.

17. Gold, H. (1971). *The Sexual Freedom League.* Paris: Olympia Press.

18. Stills, S. (1970). *Love The One You're With.* Los Angeles: Atlantic.

19. Carroll, L. (1865). *Alice's Adventures in Wonderland.* London: Macmillan.

20. Plinius, S. (112). *Letters.* Retrieved from *wikiquote.com.* Accessed Jan. 1, 2017.

21. Rousseau, J. (1754). *Discourse On Equality.* Amsterdam: Rey.

22. Anonymous. Retrieved from *quoteinvestigator.com.*

23. Max, P. Retrieved from *quotegarden.com.*

24. Easton, D. & Hardy, J. (2009). *The Ethical Slut,* 2nd ed. Berkeley, CA: Celestial Arts.

25. Anapol, D. (2010). *Polyamory in the 21st Century.* Lanham, MD: Rowman & Littlefield.

Chapter 4. Yin Versus Yang

1. Descartes, R. (1637). *Le Discours de la Methode.* Paris: Ian Maire.

2. Kant, I. (1788). *Critique of Practical Reason.* Retrieved from Project Gutenberg.

3. Orwell, G. (1949). *Nineteen Eighty-Four.* London: Secker & Warburg.

4. Huxley, A. (1932). *Brave New World.* London: Chatto & Windus.

5. Brown, D. (2003). *The Da Vinci Code.* New York: Doubleday.

6. Avid Life Media. (2016). *www.ashleymadison.com.* Alexa Internet.

7. Labriola, K. (2010). *Love in Abundance.* Eugene, OR: Greenery Press.

8. Thoreau, H. (1854). *Walden.* Boston: Ticknor and Fields.

9. Legato, M. (2005). *Why Men Never Remember and Women Never Forget.* New York: Rodale.

10. Easton, D. & Hardy, J. (2009). *The Ethical Slut,* 2nd ed. Berkeley, CA: Celestial Arts.

Chapter 5. Practical Matters

1. Moses. (BC). *King James' version of the Bible.* Retrieved from *wikisource.org.* Accessed Jan. 1, 2017.

2. Bergstrand, C. & Sinski, J. (2010). *Swinging in America.* Santa Barbara, CA: Praeger.

3. Voltaire. (1793). *Convention Nationale.* Paris: Google Books.

4. Rosenberg, S. (Director). (1967). *Cool Hand Luke.* Hollywood: Warner Brothers.

5. Reiner, R. (Director). (1992). *A Few Good Men.* Hollywood: Castle Rock.

6. Wilde, O. (1893). *A Woman of No Importance.* London: Haymarket.

7. Gould, T. (1999). *The Lifestyle.* Toronto: Random House.

8. Mazursky, P. (Director). (1969). *Bob & Carol & Ted & Alice.* Hollywood: Columbia Pictures.

9. Crystal, B. (1985). *Saturday Night Live.* New York: NBC.

10. Ray, J. (1678). *English Proverbs.* London: Retrieved from wikisource.org. Accessed Jan. 1, 2017.

11. Holland, K. (Publisher). (2016). *Penthouse Letters.* New York: PH Global Media.

12. Buffet, W. (1994). *Retrieved from wikiquote.com,* cited from an address to stockholders. Accessed Jan. 1, 2017.

13. Saint-Exupery, A. (1943). *Le Petit Prince.* Paris: Reynal & Hitchcock.

14. Blake, W. (1792). *Bartlett's Familiar Quotations.* New York: Little, Brown.

Chapter 6. Swinging and "The Lifestyle"

1. Agnes, M. ed., (2011). *Webster's New World Dictionary*. New York: Simon & Schuster.

2. Gould, T. (1999). *The Lifestyle*. Toronto: Random House.

3. Carroll, L. (1865). *Alice's Adventures in Wonderland*. London: Macmillan.

4. Kaufman, M. (Director). (2008). *American Swing*. Hollywood: Magnolia Pictures.

5. McGinley, R. (2016). *NASCA International Directory*. Retrieved from *nasca .com*. Accessed Jan. 1, 2017.

6. Browning, E. (1850). *Sonnets from the Portuguese*. Retrieved from Project Gutenberg.

7. Russell, B. (2012). *Six Degrees of Passion*. Seattle: Amazon Kindle.

8. Jong, E. (1973). *Fear of Flying*. New York: Holt, Rinehart and Winston.

9. Ritz, C. (1908). *The Phrase Finder*. Retrieved from *phrases.org*. Accessed Jan. 1, 2017.

10. Mencken, H. (1918). *In Defense of Women*. New York: Alfred A. Knopf.

11. *Ibid.*

12. Beaudrillard, J. (1987). *Cool Memories*. New York: Verso

13. Kelley, M. (Creator) (2008). *Swingtown*. New York: CBS Distribution.

14. Corbett, J. (2011). *Welcome to the Fun House*. Prescott, AZ: Nirvana.

15. Allen, W. Retrieved from *quoteland.com*.

Chapter 7. Digital Double Dating

1. Ansari, A. & Klineberg, E. (2015). *Modern Romance: An Investigation*. New York: Penguin.

2. Lady Antebellum. (2010). *Need You Now*. Los Angeles: Capitol Records.

3. Bartlett, J. (1882). *Bartlett's Familiar Quotations*. London: Little, Brown.

4. Seinfeld, J. Retrieved from *goodreads.com*. Accessed Jan. 1, 2017.

5. Hilton, P. (2016). Retrieved from *brainyquote.com*. Accessed Jan. 1, 2017.

6. Danielou, A. (1992). *Gods of Love and Ecstasy*. New York: Inner Traditions.

7. Parker, D. Retrieved from *goodreads.com*. Accessed Jan. 1, 2017.

8. Lee, A. (Director). (1997). *The Ice Storm*. Hollywood: Fox Searchlight.

9. Kubrick, S. (Director). (1999). *Eyes Wide Shut*. Hollywood: Warner Bros.

10. Ortega y Gasset, J. (1911). *Meditations on Quixote*. Urbana: University of Illinois Press.

11. Coward, N. (1931). *Mad Dogs and Englishmen*. Retrieved from *traditional-music.co.uk*. Accessed Jan. 1, 2017.

12. Millet, C. (2001). *The Sexual Life of Catherine M*. New York: Grove Press.

Chapter 8. Threesomes, Foursomes, and Moresomes

1. Voltaire. (1759). *Candide*. Paris: Cramer, et al.

2. Kaufman, P. (Director). (1990). *Henry & June*. Hollywood: Universal Pictures.

3. Curtiz, M. (Director). (1942). *Casablanca*. Hollywood: Warner Bros.

4. Mokhonoana, M. Retrieved from *goodreads.com*. Accessed Jan. 1, 2017.

5. Crosby, D. (1967). *Triad*. Los Angeles: RCA.

6. Meyers, J. (1997). *Bogart: A Life in Hollywood*. London: Andre Deutch.

7. Mazursky, P. *Ibid*.

8. Heywood, J. (1546). *Proverbs*. Retrieved from *archive.org*. Accessed Jan. 1, 2017.

9. Miller, T. (1999). *The '60s Communes: Hippies and Beyond*. Syracuse, NY: Syracuse University Press.

10. Yimou, Z. (Director). (1991). *Raise the Red Lantern*. Hong Kong: Orion Classics.

11. Kopple, B. (Director). (2005). *Havoc*. Hollywood: New Line Cinema.

12. Allen, W. (Director). (1972). *Everything You Always Wanted to Know About Sex*. Hollywood: United.

Chapter 9. Polyamory

1. Anapol, D. (2010). *Polyamory in the 21st Century*. Lanham, MD: Rowman & Littlefield.

2. Nin, A. (1976). *The Diary of Anais Nin*. New York: Harcourt Brace Jovanovich.

3. Abbot & Costello (1944). *Who's on First*. Retrieved from *archive.org*. Accessed Jan. 1, 2017.

4. Dumas, A. (1844). *The Three Musketeers*. Paris: La Siecle.

5. Labriola, K. (2010). *Love in Abundance*. Eugene, OR: Greenery Press.

Chapter 10. Friends with Benefits

1. West, M. (1928). *Diamond Lil*. Retrieved from Internet Broadway database. Accessed Jan. 1, 2017.

2. Jepsen, C. (2012). *Curiosity*. Richmond, BC: Schoolboy Records.

3. Maguire, S. (Director). (2001). *Bridget Jones's Diary*. Hollywood: Miramax.

4. Brooks, R. (Director). (1977). *Looking for Mr. Goodbar*. Hollywood: Paramount

Chapter 11. The Appeal of Non-Possessive Intimate Relationships

1. Wilder, B. (1955). *The Seven Year Itch*. Hollywood: 20th Century Fox.

2. Mieszkowski, K. (2007). "Congratulations! Your Marriage Has Expired." *Salon,* Sept. 21.

3. Shelley, P. (1821). *Epipsychidion*. London: Ollier.

4. Robbins, T. (1980). *Still Life with Woodpecker.* New York: Bantam Books.

5. Picasso, P. (undated). Retrieved from *brainyquote.com.* Accessed Jan. 1, 2017.

6. Allison, M. (1958). *Local Color.* Hackensack, NJ: Prestige.

7. King, R. (1992). (*Videotaped plea during the L.A. riots.*) Retrieved from *youtube.com.* Accessed Jan. 1, 2017.

8. Congreve, W. (1697). *The Mourning Bride.* London: Betterton's Co.

9. Reed, L. (1972). *Walk on the Wild Side.* London: RCA.

10. Teresa, M. Retrieved from *wikiquotes.com.* Accessed Jan. 1, 2017.

11. Heinlein, R. (1961). *Stranger in a Strange Land.* New York: Putnam.

12. Hall, L. Retrieved from *quotegarden.com.* Accessed Jan. 1, 2017.

13. Dylan, B. (1964). *Another Side of Bob Dylan.* New York: Columbia

14. Thoreau, H. (1840). *The Writings of Henry D. Thoreau.* Retrieved from *thoreau.library.ucsb.edu.* Accessed Jan. 1, 2017.

15. Meyers, N. (Director). (2009). *It's Complicated.* Hollywood: Universal Pictures.

16. Blake, W. (1789). *Songs of Innocence and Experience.* Retrieved from *blakearchive.org.* Accessed Jan. 1, 2017.

17. Frank, K. & DeLamater, J. (2010). "Deconstructing Monogamy." In Barker, M. & Langdridge, D., eds. *Understanding Non-Monogamies.* New York: Routledge.

18. Lennon, J. (1971). *Imagine.* New York: Apple.

Bibliography

Anapol, D. (2010). *Polyamory in the 21st Century*. Lanham, MD: Rowman & Littlefield.

Barash, P. B., & Lipton, J. E. (2001). *The Myth of Monogamy*. New York: Holt.

Barker, M., & Langdridge, D. (eds.). (2010). *Understanding Non-Monogamies*. New York: Routledge.

Bergstrand, C. R., & Sinski, J. B. (2010). *Swinging in America*. Santa Barbara, CA: Praeger.

Block, J. (2009). *Open: Love, Sex, and Life in an Open Marriage*. Berkeley, CA: Seal Press.

Constantine, L. L., & Constantine, J. M. (1973). *Group Marriage*. New York: Macmillan.

Easton, D., & Hardy, J. W. (2009). *The Ethical Slut* (2nd ed.). San Francisco: Greenery.

Ellis, A. (1972). *The Civilized Couple's Guide to Extramarital Adventure*. New York: Pinnacle.

Foster, M., Foster, B., & Hadady, L. (2000). *Three in Love*. Lincoln, NE: iUniverse.

Frank, K. (2013). *Plays Well in Groups*. Lanham, MD: Rowman & Littlefield.

Gould, T. (1999). *The Lifestyle*. New York: Random House.

Hauck, P. A. (1981). *Overcoming Jealousy and Possessiveness*. Louisville, KY: Westminster John Knox.

Labriola, K. (2010). *Love in Abundance*. Eugene, OR: Greenery Press.

Lano, K. (Ed.) (1995). *Breaking the Barriers to Desire*. AKPress.org.

Ley, D. J. (2009). *Insatiable Wives*. Lanham, MD: Rowman & Littlefield.

Margolis, J. (1973). *The Ins and Outs of Orgies*. San Francisco: Cliff House Books.

Mazur, R. (2000). *The New Intimacy*. Lincoln, NE: iUniverse.

Millet, C. (2003). *The Sexual Life of Catherine M*. New York: Grove Press.

Morgan, A. (2012). *Swinging By a Thread*. Amazon: Kindle edition.

Nearing, R. (1992). *Loving More: The Polyfidelity Primer*. Amazon: paperback.

O'Neill, N., & O'Neill, G. (1972). *Open Marriage*. New York: Lippincott.

Perel, E. (2006). *Mating in Captivity*. New York: HarperCollins.

Pines, A. M. (1998). *Romantic Jealousy: Causes, Symptoms, Cures*. New York: Routledge.

Rogers, C. (1972). *Becoming Partners: Marriage and Its Alternatives*. New York: Delacorte Press.

Ryan, C., & Jetha, C. (2010). *Sex at Dawn*. New York: HarperCollins.

Stern, D. (2013). *Swingland*. New York: Touchstone.

Talese, G. (1980). *Thy Neighbor's Wife*. New York: HarperCollins.

Taormino, T. (2008). *Opening Up*. San Francisco: Cleis Press.

Taylor, E., & Sharkey, L. (2006). *Em & Lo's Rec Sex*. San Francisco: Chronicle Books.

Thomas, P. (1997). *Recreational Sex*. Cleveland: Peppermint Publishing.

Vantoch, V. (2007). *The Threesome Handbook*. New York: Thunder's Mouth Press.

Veaux, F., & Rickert, E. (2014). *More Than Two*. Portland, OR: Thorntree Press.

Wayland-Smith, E. (2016). *Oneida: From Free Love Utopia to the Well-Set Table*. New York: Picador.

Index

About the Author

Leslie Spurr, PhD, is a relationship therapist who works with sexually adventurous couples and singles, assisting them to reconcile their atypical lifestyles with the demands and expectations of mainstream society. A licensed clinical psychologist, Dr. Spurr has been in independent practice for more than 30 years in Los Angeles, Atlanta, and Honolulu.